LIVING WITH DYING
A Family Vocation

Shoonie Hartwig

Bless

Love to You

yours !

Shoonie

DEDICATION

TO ALL OUR LOVED ONES WHO HAVE GONE BEFORE

ANNA MARVICK

MELBURN DONHOWE

JULE ZABAWA

AUDREY DONHOWE

KARL HARTWIG

JERRY HARTWIG

BETTY ANN RAMSETH

GUS DONHOWE

and

CHARLOTTE MARVICK DONHOWE

SHOONIE HARTWIG

CONTENTS

Dedication

1   Endings   1

2   The Piano Bench   8

3   Home   18

4   The Yellow Tablet   32

5   The Way We Were   48

6   There is Hope for a Tree   62

7   The Rings   79

8   Practicing   97

9   Remembering   113

10   A Song is for Singing   136

After Words

ENDINGS

A year ago Christmas, I gave the first edition of **Living with Dying** to my children, Kristopher, Kari and Kurt. Given the personal nature of this manuscript, it was important that they read it in its initial birthing.

A few days later, Kristopher told me that he needed to put it down after a few chapters but his son, Nate, picked it up right away and read it from start to finish. Finding his dad soon after, he asked, "Is this why you are a hospice doctor?"

Kristopher's reply, "I don't think so, but I do believe it has given me a capacity for my work."

Our family's particular inheritance of endings is a generational story, one that started before I was born. Although I grew up with a knowing of absence claiming me early as a fatherless child, I was living a continuum of loss. What I couldn't have understood then nor envisaged was how our many endings would become our beginnings in a generational vocation training.

As I am now in my eighth decade, the Psalm's admonition, 'teach us to number our days so we might gain a heart of wisdom' grabbed my attention. In fact, I leapt out of bed in the middle of the night to find my calculator. On August 20, 2015, I had lived **29,200** days. Until then, it had never occurred to me to count these cumulative days. Impressive. Nor had I considered how my heart might become wiser by so doing.

The number is startling. Twelve months in a year, three hundred and sixty-five days in a year are constant measuring points. But days? You can block them into their month; you can measure them by their ever-repeating twenty-four hours. But no matter how you configure them, a day is relentlessly unto itself.

Yet we try. We try to slow the too fast moving minutes; we try to escape the tediousness of relentless hours; we try to hold on to precious seconds. We try to escape a day's being on its own terms. For these many lived days, I've tried all manner of ways to time manage. Perhaps this is where wisdom begins: How not to.

I was in fourth grade, walking home from school in Northfield, Minnesota. We had all been waiting for this day since the ending of World War II. My sister Peg's fiancé, Jule, was returning from overseas at 4 o'clock that day.

Well, that was the anticipated time. This beloved member of our family had been the focus of four years waiting with Peg. She would read me excerpts from his letters that took a month of days to reach her.

So there I was, after school, trying to make my walk from Longfellow school last longer than usual. I decided that instead of walking, or running, just in case Jule came early, I would measure my steps. My horrid brown oxford shoes plodded heel to toe as the blocks moved me slowly past the hospital, the park and finally to St. Olaf Avenue and home.

My anxiety grew with each heel to toe advance. Would he be there? And, if not, WHEN? In my relatively short-lived days, my awareness of these possibilities was so present in my psyche that more often than not, I'd get sick. My stomach would knot. I'd run a temperature. Anxiety had me in its grip.

It started when I had been living **1,045** days, 51 days before my third birthday. This was the day my dad died suddenly from a heart attack. This was the day when everything changed. His presence in my life had measured my days. His leaving for work every morning, his returning every night, these were the time markers that gave each day meaning. But then time stopped. The normal ceased and I waited, and waited, and waited. I waited for normal to come back.

Living with waiting became a visceral reality. Time couldn't be trusted. I couldn't imagine how pervasive this time lock would become, not only for me but also for my extended family. I couldn't have imagined how its incessant repetitions over many years would impact generations within each household.

Ours is a very particular inheritance of loss. That is why it is only now, with 29,200 days lived that the time has come to write our story. We have an unusual legacy in untimely, sudden deaths, not just once, not just twice. Living with dying has become our family vocation.

There is nothing new under the sun about life's conundrums within joy and sadness, hope and despair, health and sickness. But life and death, living and dying? Now that's another matter. Denial doesn't cover it. In spite of its daily reality in all of life, we try our best to deny death's presence. We ignore it away; we pray it away. We try to explain its unpredictability, its ferocious possibilities. Death is to be fought for we are, after all, immortal.

The fear, the anxiety about death's presence in life and its inevitability is at the core of the inevitable question: Why? Philosophers, poets, theologians, psychologists, to name a few,

4

have wrestled with the 'why' through the ages. When untimely death occurs, the weight of this question is compounded with other issues.

This Deuteronomy verse names it: "I call heaven and earth to witness against you today that I have set before you life and death, blessings and curses. Choose life so that you and your descendants might live."

You may well wonder before reading these chapters if, indeed, as a family we have been cursed with incessant loss. Living between blessings and curses is fraught with theological and societal interpretations so much so that it leaves many clergy as well as well-intended friends uncomfortable and awkward in our presence. The silent *why* screams.

Resurrection isn't easy. Daring to live again is daring to lose again, daring to be vulnerable to the blessings and the curses of life. If we are able to face the *why*, this is the beginning. But then comes the *how* to find meaning in life once again. Is it possible that when the channels of grief gouge our souls to barren emptiness that joy, forgiveness and gratitude might deepen with the knowledge of who we are and to whom we belong? But how?

You might imagine that after 29,200 days I have mastered heel to toe time-life management skills. You might imagine that I have a 'choose life' map or pious platitudes, heaven forbid, for grieving souls. After all, if living with dying experience counts, I qualify.

What I have learned, beyond my own knowing, is how others have lived with their particular *why* question and discovered their particular ways to resurrection. As a family, we have been privileged to live within other cultural settings whether in a primarily African American church community in North Carolina or as educators in Tanzania over many years.

These were the lived spaces where we witnessed the profound courage of those whose daily lives know living with dying in societal frames of exclusion, of economic barrenness and power structures deeming some unworthy. They are the ones who have taught me that livingdying has no in between space. When exclusion from living spaces, working spaces, learning spaces determines your worth, your ability, your possibility, then livingdying is known within power structures that sustain one voice telling you not only where you cannot go but who you cannot be. The death of souls in the making.

It is my hope that as you read this chronicle, you will come to understand why my heart is full of gratitude for all who have shown me new ways to number my days, and as a family, how we have come to know living with dying as our family vocation. Our inheritance has given us a capacity to discover beginnings in endings, to choose life midst continuing revelations of being chosen.

At a recent visit with my three- year- old great-grandson, Zachary Gerald, he looked at me with a puzzled expression and asked, "Gamma, where is your papa?"

And I said,

"Everywhere."

THE PIANO BENCH

It was the summer just before my fourth birthday. My mom and I took a bus from our home in Northfield, Minnesota to visit relatives in Story City, Iowa. Aunts, uncles, cousins and grandparents all gathered to welcome us back. When we were asked, "Would you like to see your old house?" my mom reluctantly agreed.

As soon as we crossed the threshold, I let go of her hand and ran as fast as my short legs could carry me to the downstairs bathroom, shouting, "DADDY, DADDY!" And then, "Daddy?" in a smaller, bewildered voice. "Where is he? I've been waiting for him to come back. Where is he?" I wailed, inconsolable, immoveable. The empty bathroom was a memory tomb.

The year before on July 1, 1938, my forty-four-year-old father died suddenly from a massive heart attack. During that year, stories were told about our daddy. I heard them but I didn't get it.

The bathroom in our Story City house was my memory space. Every morning, he carried me in my high chair where I sat, waiting for the game to begin. He'd daub his face with the white foamy shaving suds, humming, pretending not to see me. And then, suddenly, he'd grin, turn to my expectant, "Me, too," face. A plop on my nose, another on my cheek, then a peck to my chin. Every morning, our bathroom play, just my daddy and me.

Later that summer, after returning home to Northfield, my mom and I were walking up St. Olaf Avenue. Holding hands, I looked into the clouds as she told me that daddy was surely looking down at me. Instead of receiving this news with any sense of comfort, I looked up to her and asked, "Are you going to leave me, too?"

Even in my very young world, the year had been tumultuous, marked first by my dad's death and then six weeks later, the uprooting of our family from Story City. We left all the securities, all the relatives; we left home. Everything I knew had suddenly changed, nothing was familiar; nothing felt right.

Everyone needed to leave. My sisters Peg and Betty Ann were students at St. Olaf College and singers in the St. Olaf choir. As a result, the conductor, F. Melius Christiansen, heard of our daddy's death. Remembering my mother, Charlotte Marvick, from his theory class when she attended the college, he called to offer her the possibility of teaching piano. This gave her the energy and the hope to leave our home in Story City, and uproot all of us to Northfield only six weeks after her husband's death.

My sisters had to move out of their college dormitories and join my teenage brothers, Jack and Gus, on the first floor of a rented home. Peg, Betty Ann, Mom and I scrunched into one bedroom, my brothers into an alcove off the kitchen. The second floor we rented to college students. Everyone was busy leaving. My sisters walked up the Avenue to their classes on the hill; my brothers rode their bikes across town to junior and senior high school.

This left me at home alone, waiting and watching for sightings of sisters and brothers. Not my mom. Before eight o'clock each morning, she walked the long St. Olaf Avenue blocks to campus as a prelude to a four-flight climb in Christiansen Music Hall to her piano studio. I couldn't tell time by a clock as a three-year-old, but I knew not to look for her until close to dark.

In Story City we waited to hear the car tire crunch of gravel on the driveway marking our daddy's return from a day's work in the Ford garage. Mom would have changed into fresh attire, supper would be on the stove, but first, time for the two of them to sit in the living room to recount the day. I'd wait until he'd say, "Where's my Snoony?" and then I'd run to his lap.

Although I was my mom's namesake, Charlotte Mae, this was my dad's early naming of me. He had listened to Fanny Brice's radio characterizations of 'Baby Snooks', and when the character Snoony was introduced – a somewhat impish kid – he thought it fit. When I started talking and couldn't form the 'sn', it changed to Shoonie, a love name inheritance for all my days.

Home. The focus in the Story City living room was a brick fireplace framed with bookshelves. A chair on either side, a couch facing the fireplace and an upright piano on the wall next to double glass paned doors that opened to a sunny dining room.

For my mother, a piano had been a part of her life as long as she could remember, even in this very house, for it was here where she grew up, where she learned what it meant to be family, where she first learned to make music, where she first sat on the piano bench.

The Marvick and later the Donhowe home, was a two-story house with a wrap-around porch, providing a gracious framework in which to raise a family of five children. Story City was, and continues to be, small town mid-America, a farming community where the distance between school, church, relatives and one's home is within easy walking distance. Norwegian heritage, Lutheran piety, education, community service and leadership were ingrained into the Marvick-Donhowe lineage as solidly as the oak floors in their home.

For Joseph, or Papa, as friends and his children called him, this house echoed absence since his wife Anna had died suddenly of blood poisoning. She was thirty-five. Charlotte, the fifth of their six children, was only three. Her older sisters would tell stories of their vivacious, fun-loving, spirited mother whose love and affection for her family left an inexpressible void.

As a single parent, Joseph took his family responsibilities very seriously, as he did with his many civic duties. This was a man well known within the community as a successful banker, businessman and land investor. He was highly respected as a churchman, one whose decorum of integrity and honor he faithfully lived. Papa brought safety, security and love to his children, but they would also learn how being responsible could require sacrifice.

Growing up in a motherless household meant older sisters and an aunt cared for the younger children especially during their Papa's frequent trips away from home. The piano bench became Charlotte's favorite place. Music making was continuous; everyone either sang or played instruments, whether at home, at church or at family recitals. She quickly demonstrated a talent for the keyboard.

Following her sister Ida and brother Severt's footsteps, she entered St. Olaf in 1913. When a representative from the college had come to St. Petri Lutheran church in Story City five years before, he encouraged parents to send their children to this Lutheran, Norwegian immigrant school. Joseph heard; Joseph decided. It was too late for his married eldest daughter, Olive, but the rest of his children would attend this college.

The piano became the center of Charlotte's studies but only for two years. Her brother Severt contracted tuberculosis from his St. Olaf roommate. Joseph arranged for him to be moved to a sanitarium in Denver, Colorado. He also decided that it would be best if Charlotte would leave St. Olaf to care for him. Ida, as the St. Olaf choir and band soloist, would complete her degree.

Charlotte spent the next two years housekeeping for Severt. Papa had arranged for a piano to be available in the Denver house, but her nursing duties gave her little opportunity to play. Yet, she found time for letter writing at the end of the day. Since leaving Story City for Northfield, she had corresponded with her high school sweetheart, Melburn Donhowe.

The Donhowes and Marvicks had a shared history in Story City through the church, the community, schools and music making. A distinguishing difference was in educational opportunities beyond high school. Joseph's financial resources and his commitment to his daughters as well as his son's educational opportunities set them apart.

Jack Donhowe, as he was called by everyone outside of his immediate family, had no choice but to stay in Story City, first as a cashier in the bank, and later joining his uncle in the Ford dealership. His work was his job. His passion was Charlotte and later their family. Letters written from the time she left Story City are a testament to their growing love. For Jack to stand up to Joseph Marvick not only to ask for his daughter's hand but requesting that she return home took courage. Think David and Goliath.

Charlotte and Jack married, settling into the Story City family setting. Theirs was a classic love match. His boisterous laughter and open display of affection to this sedate and reserved woman brought delight to all who witnessed it, as she'd say, 'Oh Melburn!' Within a few years of their marriage, Joseph moved out of the Marvick home, and the young couple moved in with their toddler daughters, Peg and Betty Ann.

Jack Donhowe's role outside our home was significant. He was the brother his siblings came to for counsel and loans. He was the one who could be depended upon to find his alcoholic friend at the bar and bring him home. He was the churchman who accompanied Alvin Rogness, then president of Luther Seminary, on a circuit of rural Iowa congregational visits. He was the man whose death caused a complete shutdown of businesses in Story City during his funeral.

He left a seemingly insurmountable void for all of us highlighted by insufficient financial resources. 1938 marked the height of the Depression. The small Ford garage where my dad worked with his uncle could not continue to support two families without him. The Northfield offer for

Charlotte meant an uprooting from everything she knew to be home and family. What she knew to be the norm would be transformed amidst no security of livelihood or her beloved to remind her daily how she was cherished.

In the midst of so many uncertainties, we were all being transposed from the piano bench. Each of us had new family responsibilities, changing our relationships with each other. Yet, Charlotte's musical score kept a steady disciplined walking tempo at work and at home.

The classical and romantic compositions of Bach, Mozart, Schumann and Chopin found artistic expression through her many students' hands on the keyboard and diligent repetition of responsible phrases for her children. The every Sunday hymnody of the Lutheran church fed her spirit. Saturday baking of whole wheat bread and kringla – a Norwegian sweet bread recipe from my grandmother – were at the heart of food offerings from her kitchen.

The upright Story City piano accompanied us to our living room in Northfield. Charlotte's studio at St. Olaf, however, housed two Steinway grands. We weren't friends. They had more time with my mom than I did. You could say that we were sibling rivals with their ever -present center stage place in her life. Even during the summers, she would leave home to study piano and take courses towards her degree.

From the time I was six through my early teens, I'd spend time with my sisters in their households helping with their young families as mom's study time meant leaving home. This was no hardship being farmed out but there was always this underlying sense of waiting and with it, the ever- present question, "Would she come back?"

Years later, as a senior at St. Olaf and a student in mom's Piano Pedagogy class, our first assignment was to write about the piano in our lives. To our mutual amazement, I personified the piano into a competitive presence, one I couldn't ignore. If I learned to play, this would assure me time with her at the end of the day. Piano lessons through the kitchen door became a daily routine.

Gradually, however, the bench and music making scored as I discovered a love for singing. Now I was following in my sisters' footsteps. The Ole choir sound entered my ears and my heart from the time we moved to Northfield; the mystery of melding text to voice captured my alto sensibilities. This delight in music making translated to my college major, preparing me to teach in public schools and piano at home.

The piano bench presence was a constant as we moved from rental home to rental home. Initially, the keyboard was my focus, learning the basics of music making. However, as homes and places changed, I began to associate family values with the bench. More than my mom's work -space, it gradually asserted itself as the purveyor of how to live well.

The piano bench didn't have a specific music score nor did it have a specific text. Already, we were learning as a family, that the bench basics would be transposed over the years. The original score started in Story City would not only change key, it would have different interpretations.

Transposition changes the original. The challenge is what you let go and what you keep. This we began to discover with the first beat of our family vocation composition.

HOME

You wouldn't think that a 7:50 a.m. history class could be a reason to get to class early. Seated alphabetically, Donhowe put me near the front of the class and on the aisle. As other students ambled in, one tall guy's casual gait began to catch my attention. 'Hey', he'd say, as he found his way to the 'h' row. I knew him from afar as a class leader throughout our four years at St. Olaf. But until now, our paths went different directions.

Jerry Hartwig was one of those guys everyone liked. His easy-going manner, his friendly banter seemed to be quite gender inclusive. At least that's what I observed and heard as two of my best friends had recently asked him out for a Sadie Hawkins Dance.

As weeks went on, the 'Hey' gradually changed, maybe a tap on the shoulder, or a brief comment on the day. Between my friends telling me details of their dates and our three-times-a-week class encounter, Jerry was hard to ignore.

When he called to ask me out, I was surprised, well, sort of. What remains in my memory as vividly as the booth where we sat for dinner, was laughter. This was one crazy, dry-witted guy whose humor was so quietly delivered, you might miss it. I didn't. From November 6, 1957 on, we were a 'senior couple'.

Jerry's parents came from Brush, Colorado for graduation. I had already met them as the Ole choir tour took us to Denver. Jerry had told them they needed to drive the ninety miles to hear and to meet. My mom had met Jerry rather regularly as I lived at home the second semester of my senior year.

When we announced our engagement, it didn't seem to surprise anyone. A wedding in a year, but first I had financial debts to clear. I accepted a position as music supervisor for five elementary schools in Red Wing, Minnesota and Jerry entered the high school scene as a history teacher in Sparta, Wisconsin.

In December of that year, 1957, my mom boarded a Greyhound Bus to attend one of my Christmas concerts. To her delight, a colleague, Agnes Larson, from St. Olaf's history department, was headed in the same direction for a professional meeting. As they told us later, after exchanging family and departmental news, Agnes asked about her former history student advisee.

"Tell me," she asked, "what does Gerald plan to do after he and Shoonie are married?" Mom's response indicated graduate school in counseling, probably at a university in Colorado.

Jerry's liberal arts majors changed annually during his four years at St. Olaf. Dr. Larson only knew him briefly as he entered the history department as a senior. So it is no wonder that her response was this.

"You know, there's a Master of Arts in Teaching degree offered at Harvard University. Colorado is good, but perhaps Harvard is better. Tell Gerald to see me the next time he's in Northfield." Maybe he'd be ready for another major change?

Never underestimate a conversation between two women on a bus.

When Jerry and I married the following June, we also wed our Northfield, Minnesota and Brush, Colorado families. Faith and Walt Hartwig had raised their three children with similar values of faith, family, education and civic responsibility. However, our small town, and mid-and western U.S. shaping would soon have new transpositions.

Three days after our 1958 June wedding, Jerry and I embarked on a road trip from Minnesota to Massachusetts. We knew nothing about Boston to say anything of Harvard. We left corn stalks, small towns, cows and German-Scandinavian heritage to enter an historical city of diverse population with an intellectual environment that sizzled.

When a fellow student in the Master of Arts in Teaching Program invited us to a debate at Harvard Law School, we quickly accepted. Josh, a dapper African American from New York City and Jerry, the casual, long-legged student from the other side of the Appalachian Mountains, discovered they were both outliers. The majority of students in their class were Ivy Leaguers. Suspect with regard to their intellectual abilities, Josh and Jerry were also viewed as bereft of any cultural heritage.

One evening, Josh joined us for a meal in our sparse two-room Cambridge apartment. "Have you ever heard of Malcolm Little?" he asked.

"Who?" We asked in complete ignorance. Little did we know how transformative this man would become, not only in the U.S. but internationally. In 1957, as a young Black Muslim, a self-taught intellectual, a civil rights activist, he would have transformative experiences causing him to change his last name to 'X'. But we didn't know that then.

"A debate is scheduled at Harvard Law School between Little and a lawyer with the NAACP. It could be interesting. With the Civil Rights movement and Dr. King's leadership, it might be a little contentious," said Josh. "Little is Muslim. Want to go?"

"Why not?" we replied.

Entering the law school atrium, we discovered the hall already crowded. At each exit, young African American men stood, clad in black, arms crossed as if at attention. The majority of the audience was similarly attired. There were few white folk.

When the debaters entered the stage, all exit doors shut. An eerie sense of anticipation pervaded. And then the words began to fly. First, the NAACP lawyer began to speak in persuasive and conciliatory tones, his tone sometimes rising to a higher pitch and then backing away. I knew this rhythmic pulse, this intonation and crescendo in music. Not in speech.

When Malcolm Little responded the difference was electric. He spoke incisively; his intonation had an edge. It was pointed, not invitational; it was accusatory, not conciliatory. His angry discourse escalated as the debate continued.

The Civil Rights movement was just beginning. The non-violent approach to change embodied in the NAACP and Dr. Martin Luther King, Jr.'s position was not in agreement with the Muslim-Malcolm Little stance. There was nothing from home, school, church, community, nothing to prepare me for this encounter.

The words that flew back and forth were not in my vocabulary. Not only had I seldom heard them, I certainly had not articulated them:

inclusion-exclusion, integrate-separate, violence-nonviolence, Christian-Muslim. It went on and on – The Nation of Islam, Elijah Muhammad, Marcus Garvey, Uncle Tom, Martin Luther King, Jr. My ignorance was profound. I could have been in physics class.

Twenty -six years later, when I taught **The Autobiography of Malcolm X** to college students in an all white-cornstalk setting, the majority of them were as unaware of these issues as I had been. When I heard Malcolm X at Harvard, it was an event. I was present, and then I quickly exited, leaving it all behind. That's what I thought.

Following completion of his Harvard degree, Jerry was hired to teach in a Boston suburban high school where he had interned as a social studies teacher. On a chilly January day in 1961, he came into the kitchen where I was nursing Karl, our one-month old son, as our eighteen-month-old Kristopher played with Matchbox cars on the linoleum floor. Our young family. Secure at home.

Without any hesitation, he enthusiastically put an innocent flyer in front of me and said, "Guess what? There's an amazing program just announced out of Columbia University called 'Teachers for East Africa'. Kenya, Tanganyika and Uganda will soon be independent, and they need English speaking teachers. Imagine! Africa!"

I was speechless and certainly not imagining. We had talked about teaching overseas when we were first married, but not now. Not with two little ones. My, "You've got to be kidding!" response was met with, "Well, with kids, we'd probably not be considered, but why not apply anyway? Just think about it. There'd be so much to learn!"

"But you said this is about TEACHING!" I exclaimed. I got that look of raised eyebrows. Probably just as well that I let it go. I didn't have words. We had entered an unknown space of possibility that within a few short months translated to certainty. We were among the 150 teachers selected. Imagine.

It's good that I couldn't imagine our new lives. Jerry left in June with all of the teachers headed for orientation at the University of Makerere in Kampala, Uganda. The plan. I would fly with our boys and meet him there. Because so many secondary schools in Tanganyika, Uganda and Kenya were mission initiatives, we had been asked if we would agree to a church assignment. Presumably, we had a natural fit given Lutheran presence was well established in Tanganyika. A missionary who received our name agreed to coordinate our school assignment with Teachers for East Africa officials. So far, so good. A plan.

A prop plane, two babes, a double-decker stroller and a carry-on-everything bag. It had to do for the five long days and nights. Eternal.

24

Kristopher, not yet two, stood like a sentinel guard by our possessions in the multiple airports en route as I would hustle with Karl into the ladies room. When we finally landed on Kampala's tarmac runway, there stood the six- foot plus Jerry. Kristopher, sighting his Dad, began running as fast as his short legs could carry him. If I could, I'd have done the same.

Within a week, all the teachers had a school assignment. All, that is, except the Hartwigs. It seemed that said missionary had forgotten his agreement. Nonetheless, we were put on a train with the assurance that once we reached Moshi, Tanganyika, we would be met and our new home awaiting us.

It took three days in a train moving so slowly we could have walked. Scrunched together in a sleeping car with two small bunk beds, we did our best. Mind you, this was pre-pampers and a food venue offering few choices. There was nothing familiar anywhere. Not in sights, smells, tastes or sounds.

Disheveled and weary, we finally stood on the train platform near Moshi. A young man met us with these German accented welcoming words: "We heard you were coming here to teach, but we have no vacancy, no room. But, we will call the head of school near Arusha. Surely, they can take you." Within an hour, we were hustled into a taxi. The driver spoke no English; we spoke no Swahili.

The car rattled its way over potholes causing the parents of two young ones to hold on tightly. Suddenly, Kristopher yelled, "LOOK!" pointing his short arm towards giraffe in the distance. Before long, zebra entered our panoramic view with towering Mt. Kilimanjaro in the background. It was a blessed relief from concerns over our future too huge to name.

Hours later the car finally shuddered to a stop. It looked like we were in the middle of a cow pasture. A group of boys were kicking a makeshift ball around. My raised eyebrow query to Jerry got this reply, "soccer." We were summarily ushered out of the taxi leaving us in a cloud of dust as it quickly sped away. Two parents, two babes, two suitcases. In the distance, we sighted a house and began to walk.

Our unannounced, sudden appearance seemed to cause no concern. For two weeks we were housed with Ilboru Secondary School's headmaster and his family of four. This Lutheran school had no teacher needs, either, but we were assured that somehow, this would all work out. Jakob and Agnes Aano, Norwegian missionaries, welcomed us so warmly that somehow the question, "WHY DID WE COME HERE?" kept at a murmur.

After two weeks, an answer. Due to health problems, one teacher suddenly returned to the States. Wonderful. Jerry could teach. The next challenge, however, regarded our housing. We were joining teachers from Canada, Norway, Great Britain, Tanganyika and the U.S. All expatriates were living in housing up the hill from the school. The Tanganyikan and Asian teachers were housed down below, separate from the rest. Would we join them? We would.

When does a house become a home? A wood stove, kerosene lanterns, intermittent running water, a porch welcoming bats and lizards, dogs barking all night, daily milk delivery in beer bottles with tobacco leaf stoppers, melismatic calls to prayer from the town Mosque before daybreak. Nothing familiar.

Everything was new and different. Arriving in August we discovered a new cold. I had thought the tropics, the southern hemisphere translated to hot or warm temperatures. But at 4,000 feet elevation at the foot of Mt. Meru and with two seasons of dry and wet, the cold-rainy season had us shivering. Sweatshirts in the tropics? Yes!

Food preparation took forever. Navigating roadside offerings of tomatoes and onions with my bungling Swahili became a daily language opportunity. Water. If my boys drank it unboiled, they could get jiardia. If they ran outside barefoot, they could get worms. If a mosquito got inside their bed nets, they could get malaria. Don't ask about snakes. Morning, noon and night, the possibilities were ever present.

Teaching or learning? The lessons were unlike any I'd known, to say nothing of imagined. Scarcity and abundance, joy and sorrow, life and death were ever present. Maasae women carrying one bucket of water on their heads for their day's needs, the sudden death of a neighbor's toddler for no explicable reason, awareness of my whiteness wherever I went were stark reminders that I was a very long way from home.

Then there was teaching. The 140 young men attending Ilboru Secondary school came from all parts of the country to study in English, their third language, and to learn about other parts of the world so that they could pass the Cambridge Examination.

One of the British legacies to a soon to be independent Tanzania was their educational system. Controlled through the Ministry of Education, secondary school curriculum and examination protocol was a British replica. Not only would the language of instruction be English, the world to be studied would be European based. Not a word anywhere about Africa.

Examinations would be written in the UK and then sent to all their protectorates and colonies as students throughout their world would take the same examination; the answer sheets were provided and pass – fail scores determined. The results would irrevocably change the lives of all who entered this educational system. It is no surprise that the students would go on strike if they believed any teacher was not preparing them well enough for the Cambridge. Too much was at stake.

Outside of the classroom, it was music that began to teach me about home. When we were told of a piano's availability, we were first in line. Within a short time, Ilboru students began queuing outside our front door after classes, waiting for a lesson on the bench. Their goal: to play a four-part hymn. The singing at daily school *sala (chapel),* and at our nearby Lutheran church, always in parts, always in a joy filled spirit, captured me. In those settings, there was no space between us.

After completing the two- year teaching contract, Jerry discovered there was no space between him and his students either. We had come to realize that we were beginning to live into a new understanding of home. The environmental challenges midst being very, very white in a very, very black world could have kept us on the fringe. But we kept getting pulled into places of belonging, in classrooms, in church, in friendships. Places that were giving us new meaning to doing justice, living kindly and walking humbly.

When Dr. Anza Lema, the first Tanzanian to head a secondary school, asked Jerry to extend his contract so that they might forge a solid foundation for Ilboru's position as a leading church educational institution, we agreed. We returned to the States a year and a half later. Now we were a family of five as infant daughter Kari joined us. Her dual citizenship was good for eighteen years.

No longer was Jerry wondering what he should do or be. He didn't leave his heart or mind in Tanzania. Rather, he entered graduate school at Indiana University to focus on African Studies with the hope that one day, he could teach about this world he had come to love. I, too, would become a student in ethnomusicology and music education at the master's level.

When it came time for Jerry to determine his dissertation topic, he was drawn to an unusual clay doll history tradition on the island of Ukerewe in Lake Victoria, Tanzania. He submitted his proposal to Ford Foreign Area Scholarship Program. This grant supported our family of five to live on this sequestered island for eight months.

It wasn't all new in that we had our three and a half Arusha years in our memories. By now Kristopher was nine, Karl eight and Kari five. Yet, in this new space, all of us were students. I home schooled the kids each morning. In the afternoon, we would often join Jerry as he interviewed those elders whose memories held the history of their ethnic family, the Bakerebe.

Using my Indiana University ethnomusicology course as background, I began recording music on tape. During our kids' free time they were happily collecting butterflies, bush whacking, or playing with Indian and Tanzanian children. Our world was quite small in this seventy-mile long and ten-mile wide island. We lived in a house built for the former manager of the local cotton ginnery. Even with a smoky wood stove and a warm kerosene refrigerator, it didn't take long for this new place to become home.

All of us were discovering. For Jerry, sitting at the feet of elders whose wisdom and knowledge of history and customs were in memory, in words spoken, changed his whole idea of becoming an historian in a global world. For me, it became the genesis space of my writing. Whether hearing new music traditions or discovering a southern hemisphere night sky, lessons of same and different were unending. New seeds were planted that would sink deeply into all of us changing forever how we would discover home.

THE YELLOW TABLET

After completion of Jerry's dissertation, he received an appointment to Duke Universities history Department as an African historian. This took us to Durham, North Carolina in 1970, now with four kids as Kurt joined us our last year in graduate school. The South. The land of magnolias, sweet potato pie and 'how y'all doin'?

When we joined the Church of the Abiding Savior Lutheran, we found a church home that brought connection to our previous chapters. This predominantly African American congregation welcomed us in mind, body and spirit. Once again, however, we were the unusual white folk. For our kids, finding connections wasn't easy since church members came from all parts of Durham.

Gradually, an idea began to find life. Might we develop a street theater program for our teenagers using African and African American resources in poetry, folk tale, song and dance? Many of our church members were active in the civil rights movement. They were keenly aware of how little their children knew about their own heritage, whether it was historical or poetical. And we were fresh from Ukerewe, appalled at the exclusion of Africa in our sons' history classes.

Possibilities were printed for everyone to read. A sampling might include Langston Hughes' 'Temptation Tale' and 'Cracker Prayer,' Sojourner Truth's 'Ain't I a Woman?' Paul Lawrence Dunbar's 'I know what the caged bird feels,' Gwendolyn Brooks' 'Children of the Poor', Richard Rive's, 'Where the Rainbow Ends'.

Then each teen began to choose a poem or a tale but also a dance, a song, a mime. Singing spirituals they knew, but these words, these stories from their own heritage, this was a first. And then to give their own voice to another's words, words that they lived, words their souls recognized was to birth a new awareness not only of their own creative abilities but pride in their rich heritage.

As the script- writer, I would sketch narration ideas on a yellow tablet keeping it perched on top of the refrigerator. What finally emerged was a story telling setting. A narrator sat in a rocking chair with several of our youngest kids at her feet, listening as she wove the program together.

In 1973, we were ready to perform "Are You Listening?" for our congregation. Gloria Cardwell, a tall black woman with a husky contralto and me, a tall white woman with my Ole mezzo, stood in front, draped in long black dresses, singing alternate verses to "Wade in the "Water," as the teenagers entered, clad in jeans and dashikis. Gloria's brother John Prince, who is now internationally known as John P. Kee, rocked the piano as everyone waded in.

This folk tale from Ukerewe, "Enkwambu and Enkende" comes from a remote island where everyone, seemingly, looks alike. I put the text into a rhyme making it very mime adaptable. Enkwambu, the black -faced monkey, played by Karl and Enkende, the white- faced lizard played by his black friend, Warrick, challenged the audience, at first.

Enkwambu and Enkende

I have a little story that I think you will like

About a monkey who is black and a lizard who is white

Enkwambu, the monkey, was walking one day

When he met Enkende, the lizard, so he stopped to say

"Listen, my friend, come to my house and eat —

I promise I'll fix you a very special treat!"

34

With delight the lizard asked, "When will this be"

And Enkwambu, the monkey, said – "Tomorrow, I'm free."

The monkey hurried home to tell his wife

Cause they'd never fed a lizard in their entire life!

The monkey said, "Lizards like intestines of a fish."

His wife said, "You really thing THAT'S a tasty dish?"

The monkey said, "I'm off to see our chief, for I'm sure he'll agree

To make our friend the lizard part of our family!"

When the lizard arrived the next day to dine,

Everything was prepared especially fine

The chair, the table, everything was set

If only the chief's rules could be easily met.

The monkey said, "Friend, I'm sure you'll agree—

Good friends are just part of one big family!

My chief said you can become one of us

If you'll eat in a chair, without too much fuss!"

So the lizard tried – and he tried – and he tried some more

But he ALWAYS landed – on the floor.

Sadly, the lizard went home.

Later that week, the monkey was walking one day

And he met the lizard, who stopped to say –

"Listen, my friend, come to MY house and eat –

I promise I'll fix you a very special treat!"

With delight the monkey asked, "When will this be?"

Enkende, the lizard, said -"Tomorrow, I'm free!"

The lizard hurried home to tell HIS wife,

Cause they'd NEVER fed a monkey in their entire life!

The lizard said, "Monkeys think corn is good food!"

His wife said, "If I told you what I think, you'd say that I'm rude!"

The lizard said, "I'm off to see our chief, for I'm sure he'll agree

To make our friend the monkey part of our family."

When the monkey arrived the next day to dine,

Everything was prepared especially fine.

The chair, the table, everything was set

If only the chief's rules could be easily met.

The monkey sat happily, ready to eat

The corn prepared especially as a tasty treat.

The lizard said, "Friend, I'm sure you'll agree –

Good friends are just part of one big family!

My chief said you can become one of us –

Just make your face white – like MINE – without too much fuss!"

So the monkey washed, and he washed, and he scrubbed his face sore.

But alas, he was just as black as before.

Now my friends, it is obvious to see

That God's been very busy, creating you and me!

The question is – DO we belong – to one big family?

Kerebe Folk Tale

Word spread and invitations began pouring in. For the next six years, we gave performances in churches, at racism conferences, for organizational meetings taking us out of state. The power of our teens telling this story was finding receptive audiences. For Lutherans, this meant primarily white folk. God was indeed 'troubling the waters'.

This included my home congregation, St. John's Lutheran in Northfield. As we had been invited to present "Are You Listening?" to the church council of the American Lutheran Church in Minneapolis, St. John's also invited us. They had never seen, heard nor fed so many black folk in their entire lives. This included Charlotte, my mom, who graciously welcomed everyone, strongly supporting her youngest.

During the early years of "Are You Listening?" the yellow tablet did what I intended it to do, received my scribbling texts. The themes of courage, hope and love seemed balanced with despair, death and emptiness. Gradually, however, this began to change. The prevalence of death throughout our poetic selections started to intrude into my writing and thinking. Once it gained space in my head, it bled into my heart and soul. Morning, noon and night, it was there; I could think of nothing else.

I began to look at the yellow tablet with dread, for it seemed to have its own voice. It seemed as if it were saying, "You need to write your own words about living and dying."

What? Followed by an equally insistent, why?

Was this because of sudden family deaths during this same time period? My brother-in-law Jule had died from a heart attack soon after our move to Durham. He and Peg had sung their way into the church and civil rights world in Washington, D.C. Not only could his liquid baritone voice hush any crowd, the two of them performed and recorded 'The Union' and 'The Confederacy' with the National Symphony. His death left Peg single parenting Kava, Mary and Kristin and the challenge of financial sustenance. Jule was 54.

As a family, we gathered; we mourned; we remembered; we sang, "For all the saints".

Five years later, Jack's wife Audrey died from cancer. Mother of six, wife of my brilliant physicist and theologian brother, she taught public school music while managing her household with steadfast love. If there were a Lutheran saint list, she'd be there. Audrey was 49.

As a family, we gathered; we mourned; we remembered; we sang, "For all the saints".

And then we all returned to our respective homes. A year after Audrey's death, I wrote the following letter to Jerry's parents in March 1976.

Sorry about long absent, silent letters from these parts.

Somehow the tempo of February and March accelerated sufficiently to

get me going in more directions than usual. The result, if anything, is

organized confusion.

I'll start with Jer. He got home at midnight last night from

the International Studies Center. Today is the deadline for all

National Endowment for Humanities proposals and he's ultimately

responsible. This was to have been spring break, just not for this

household. Today, President Sanford hosts a big conference at Duke;

Jerry represents International Studies.

At long last, I got Jerry to a doctor. This has not been an

easy year stress-wise and it has taken a toll without a doubt. More

tests next week including the usual heart radiology. One thing is

already clear, he's going to be put on a diet plus prescribed exercise.

After Lenten service this week, Jer asked the kids, seemingly in jest,

'So, thought of what to give up for Lent?' Karl looked at him and

said, "Stop saying yes to everyone who wants you to do a job!" Good

old Karl – tell it like it is!

Speaking of, he's GROWING…the old sturdy bod is

lengthening out and he loves it! School…he's generally turned

off…hates French with a passion but likes teachers sufficiently to

work a bit but not much. He seems to get along better, and this is certainly reflected at home. Take your pluses where you can get them!

Kari has sort of come to a standstill height wise. She wants to go out for track so goes for a physical next week. She's finally found her niche in the classroom – a small group of girls and they get together fairly often for slumber parties, etc., all of which is a totally new experience for her. Needless to say, the result is HAPPY to see.

Kris takes track VERY seriously. He's running his 7 and 8 miles a day but not doing it well, so he says. He hears about Governor's School the 15th of April. He was nominated in math and choir but the selection committee put him the math category since you can only go in one field. He's made the first two cutoffs. Competition is stiff as seventy kids were nominated just from his high school…then the city…to the county before state finalists are selected.

Kurt could fill up a whole page so I'll try and condense. First, the child reads like a third or fourth grader – blows our minds – reads EVERYTHING and fluently –all because of Spidey comics ala Electric Company. His best friend, Bruce White from across the road, is the same way. The two of them are something else.

As for me – we perform, "Are You Listening?" in Greensboro in two weeks for a racism conference. Several of the teen girls wanted to add new dances. Then I thought it would be good to rearrange the program adding other new things, like a new folk tale, around themes of identity — who are you, where are you going — who are you in community and how do you live out the above. So that means I'm rewriting the whole narration.

Next week, Jerry leads a conference at Duke on the role of disease in history. John Rowe from Northwestern is coming. He and his family were in Uganda when we were on Ukerewe and we stayed with them during a history conference at the University of Makerere. John comes Thursday and is here for supper. Friday, we host a buffet dinner for the fourteen plus conference folk. Sometime that evening, 'cousin' Merle comes to join us and stay. Saturday morning, I teach piano as usual. Saturday night, it's just John and Merle and then I go to orchestra rehearsal with Durham Choral Society as we have a concert Sunday.

Sunday, John leaves and not too sure about Merle's departure. Sunday afternoon, I rehearse with kids at church and then scoot to Page Auditorium at Duke for our choral concert. Jerry just told me that Henry Ferguson called (publisher of my book, THE BOOK AND THE DRUM) so he and his wife will be here Monday for dinner. Needless to say, I'm planning menus since I have piano students 'til late afternoon.

My Mom turns 80 on April 1st. My sister Betty Ann has started making arrangements for a Donhowe family gathering. Jack and Aud's daughter, Maren, will be married late May, so Mom's

gala will be the week of the wedding. Getting everyone there will be a

challenge, but more than worth it.

Can't wait to welcome you Brush g'parents! Maybe Jer's book

will be in hand when you're here!! Love to all

S J and K's

Our lives were full and well. *The Book and the Drum* had been published in a series Jerry initiated for middle school readers. I used the metaphor of the book to illustrate the impact and tension between education, missionaries and traders within the Ukerewe island setting and the drum representing traditional ways of knowing. Brief vignettes of many informants for Jerry's research were introduced, illustrating the inevitable conflicts caused by outside intrusion.

Jerry's book, *The Art of Survival* not only showcased the role of oral tradition in historical research but he ushered in a critical awareness of the historian's role in documenting memory yet to find life on the printed page. As one of his informant's eloquently put it, "Words that are spoken fly like the wind. Words that are written live forever."

You'd think with all of this activity, the yellow tablet would quietly stay where it belonged – on top of the refrigerator. Not so. My response was inching from ignoring to irritating to an anxious premonition. One day,

I tuned into a poetry reading on public radio, and all the readings focused on dying. My niece handed me Anne Morrow Lindberg's book, *Hour of Lead, Hour of Gold*. Everywhere I turned, it was there, stalking me.

This was more than Jule and Audrey's death. What did it mean? I began to look up at the refrigerator with dread. I was convinced that I was going to die. It seemed the only reason for this increasing dread, this weighting of my soul in fear. I couldn't speak about it to anyone. I dared not give it life.

At times, I could hardly breathe. Finally, one morning, I looked up at the top of the refrigerator. It was time. I grasped the yellow tablet, and picked up my pen. This is what I wrote.

What is it to live and to die?

There is death in every day. Despairs and fears. Fear over our jobs, our children, our finances, our friends, our loneliness, our marriage – our future.

Despairs that drown out life.

If God did indeed become flesh and dwell among us for all time, how are we to know?

Spirit is alive in words and music, in laughter and in smiles, in flowers and in butterflies, in forgiveness and in friendship, in handclasps – in love.

Yet in death, we shut away our hearing ears and seeing eyes – our touching and caring – our growing – all our sources of creative being.

Yet it is in this dying that we see our meaning, for the eternal Spirit can spring to life if there is someone who can love us enough that we dare risk life once again.

This is resurrection – the rebirth of hope – that in all death, we experience life – that when we are able – we hold out our hand to our brothers and sisters in their despair – giving them a glimpse of that greater love that allows us to do so.

This is life – that in the Spirit of Jesus – despair cannot overcome.

Could it be that from the seeds of suffering and oppression, rejection and utter desolation, springs an inner, stronger compassion, joy and hope? For our roots have sunk deeper into the knowledge of who we really are – to whom we really belong.

Could it be that the desert will really blossom?

When I finished, I put the pen down, exhausted. It felt as if this weight, this inexplicable mass of words had been physically expelled out of my body. It was as if I had been in labor and finally birthed these words. What had been growing within me was now alive.

On the yellow tablet.

When Jerry came home for lunch that day, I was still sitting at the table, the tablet in front of me. "What's happening?" he asked. I handed him the tablet as I crawled onto his lap weeping, not with tears of relief, but with tears filled with, 'Why'?

THE WAY WE WERE

Over the next weeks, my anxiety about dying receded. The writing

had birthed a new calm in my heart and soul. There was so much

happening in our family, my attention gratefully returned to a focus on our

living. Jerry was teaching at Duke and continuing his African research

projects. My piano bench was busy, teaching more than thirty students a

week.

Each of the kids was thriving in their very particular ways. Between

all of their lives, Jerry's, and mine – not to mention "Are You Listening?" –

our lives were full of discovery, full of possibilities, full of imagination.

There was a sense of security and meaning in all of this.

One of the best plans Jerry and I worked out was to send each of

the kids, once they turned sixteen, to spend six weeks with their Hartwig

grandparents in Brush, Colorado. Not only did they have the experience of

being an only child, they were spoiled royally. The relationship developed by each of them is reflected in this letter written by Karl in March 1977, after his Grandparent visit.

Dear Grandma

Hope everything is going ok and you get out of the hospital soon.

Everything at home is going smoothly. We now have a dog named Simba which everyone likes. I don't have to clean up after, yet at least. Kurt was supposed to but of course Mom ended up doing it. I take him to the vet for shots and things otherwise it's great having him.

Dad came back from Sudan in good spirits. He met my friend Moses there. Moses is going to be coming to the States with some Americans from Queens College in New York. He's planning to finish his education here. Hopefully, I'll find some way to get in contact with him while in the States.

Schools getting to be more of a good thing. I'm doing better in my work and get along with all of my teachers. Kari, Kris and Kurt are doing well to.

I have a job now at a restaurant named Marios. I bus tables and wash dishes. It's a lot of fun because a lot of my good friends work there. Kris burned his hand with hot grease at work and had to go to the emergency room. He's alright now though.

I'm looking forward to the summer with all the family and going to the mountains. I hope to do some fishing there if possible. Say hi to Grandpa. Love you both.

Dear Grandma

Hope everything is going ok. and you get out of the hospital soon.

Everything at home is going smoothly. We now have a dog named Simba which everyone likes. I don't have to clean up after yet at least, Kurt was supposed to but of course mom ended up doing it. I take him to the vet for shots and things other wise its great having him.

Dad come back from Sudan in good spirits. He met my friend Moses there. Moses is going to be coming to the states with some americans from Queens College in New York. He's planning to finish his education here. Hopefully I'll find some way to get in contact with him while in the states.

Schools getting to be more of a good thing. I'm doing better in my work and get along with all of my teachers. Kari, Kris, & Kurt are doing well to.

Karl's reference to his job as bus boy at a nearby Italian restaurant was a key ingredient in his growing confidence in and out of school. Not only did he enjoy his fellow workers, this new role of employee with responsibilities seemed to add inches to his sense of well - being. The owners of Mario's restaurant had a cabin near the ocean. As a thank you to their employees, periodically several would be invited for a weekend. When Karl received an invitation, he could hardly contain himself.

It was a big day. Charlotte was visiting and joined the rest of us to wave Karl off with his fellow worker, Duane, driving his father's car. Having completed their afternoon shift, they picked up friend Danny and set out on the four-hour drive to the coast in hopes that they'd arrive at the cabin before dark. Karl's delight in this trip was underscored in that it was the first time ever that he was off, by himself, away from family and home with his friends.

Kristopher had gone out with several high school buddies that evening, so when the doorbell rang about 1 a.m., I stumbled out of bed, thinking that he'd forgotten his key. Opening the door to two policemen, their car in our driveway, lights still whirling, I stood transfixed.

"Mrs. Hartwig?"

I nodded, speechless.

"Would you get your husband, please?"

When Jerry and I returned, the words, "There's been an accident," simply didn't, simply couldn't register. Accident? Evidently, Duane, Karl and Danny needed a gas stop. When they got back on the highway, Duane misjudged a truck coming around a curve. The impact of the crash killed Duane and Karl instantly. Danny, who had just switched seats with Karl into the back, survived.

Within those words, "There's been an accident," within that moment, I became Lot's wife, encased in a salt pillar. I *shut my seeing eyes, my hearing ears, my feeling heart.* I tried to keep the words from coming into the house, but they couldn't be held back.

When Kris came home, Jerry had to tell him. Later, he had to tell Kari. And then there was Charlotte, who didn't awaken during those harrowing hours of police presence and neighbors gathering. She came into the living room, ready for her usual 8 o'clock coffee to be greeted by many folks already gathered. And then there was Kurt, who was spending the night with his friend Bruce across the road.

The date was August 5, 1977. Karl was sixteen years old.

This living nightmare had no end. Family began to arrive. Friends filled our house. Phone calls had to be made, a service planned. I went through the required greetings, preparing food, answering calls, but it wasn't me. It was the pillar around my body, shielding me. Somehow, the sun kept rising and setting as the days unfolded, each with the increasing knowledge that the words – "there's been an accident" – not only crossed the threshold of the front door, they were in his room, in the kitchen, in the laundry. They were there to stay.

In this new reality, Karl would never walk through the door, never call, "HEY, I'm home!" I'd never see that sweet, smiley face again. This simply couldn't be.

Stay in the pillar.

There was no present, no future, only past. An airless void. I went through all the formalities that were required during those first days. Every dawn's first light was too terrifying. Retreat. Retreat to the numb pillar where I only looked back to stability and security, to Karl, alive. The way we were.

My body was totally unpredictable. When I could feel the steady rise of sobs that could not be quelled, I'd run to the shower, turn on the spigot full blast in hopes that it would drown the gut wrenching wails that spewed out with such force that it seemed as if I was turning inside out.

One day, even with so many people in our small ranch house, my mother came up to me, put her hands on my shoulders and said firmly yet quietly, "You still have a race to run." Only those words. Somehow they crept into my soul and would keep resurfacing in the years to come.

Karl's service at Abiding Savior was marked with hymns, spirituals, words and tears. I couldn't sing; I couldn't cry. If I started, the pillar would dissolve and me with it. Afterwards, all of our extended family gathered at our home. It was quiet; the notably boisterous family laughter of my brothers and sisters could not to be heard.

Jerry said, looking at me, "I need to hear what you wrote on the yellow tablet."

I went to the refrigerator and brought it to him. Someone else read it, I can't remember. What I do remember is that as I listened to my words, I thought: "I did die!"

Later Jerry would ask one of his students to write it in calligraphy. When she asked, "How shall I sign it?" he said, "Karl's mother."

Within a few days, everyone left, returning to the stability and security of their own homes and families. Now it was just us – Kristopher, Kari, Kurt, Jerry and me. Our new family. Somehow, we all went through the motions. This first week in August had changed everyone's sense of who we were not just as a family group, but each one of us individually.

In two weeks, Kris would leave home for his first year at St. Olaf. Entering such a totally different community, leaving family behind was a gift of space away from the rest of us. In this new environment, he didn't have to be reminded of the way we were.

That left Kari, suddenly the oldest, the one on whom her father and I would rely more and more. We called her our "Rock of Gibraltar." She knew when phone calls were too much, when knocks on the front door required a kind, "they're not available now," or, upon seeing either Jerry or me too sad to move, she'd wrap her arms around us and hold on. She shouldered emotional responsibilities far beyond her thirteen years.

Then there was seven-year-old Kurt. Within two short weeks, his oldest brother left home and his other brother died. It was too much. Night after night, he crawled into Karl's bed, huddling under Karl's favorite jean jacket. Barely able to say the words, he cried, "I just want him to come back once, just once, so I can say goodbye."

He was desperately trying to make sense out of it. One day, he came home from second grade with several small pieces of paper stapled together. When he came into the house, he went into the family room and sat by the fireplace, paging through these little pages.

"What is that?" I asked. "Did you make something in school?"

He looked up and said very somberly, "I wrote a book," and handed it to me. This is what he wrote:

My Brother Died

My brother died in a car wreck. He was with two other boys. It was Dwain's fault they died. Dwain was my brothers friend my brother's name is Karl Walter Hartwig. There was one more boy his name is Danny he got to live but Karl and Dwain died. Karl and Dwain worked at Marios. Its an Italian reserant and Danny worked at Lowes. My name is Kurt Gerald Hartwig. My mother's name is Shoonie May and my father's Gerald Hartwig. My brother's name is Kris Hartwig and my sister's name is Kari Agnes Hartwig. My friend is Bruce. He was the first child who knew about it but he didn't tell me my parents told me it was Saturday when I got the bad news. I was troubled all morning long.

ABOUT THE AUTHER Kurt Hartwig is in 2nd grad I am Kurt Hartwig

It's very troublesome when someone in your family dies

This is a true book about my brother and his friend. I think you would have cried too if Karl was your brother and died. I hope you do not cry when you read this book. I am very glad to share this book with you.

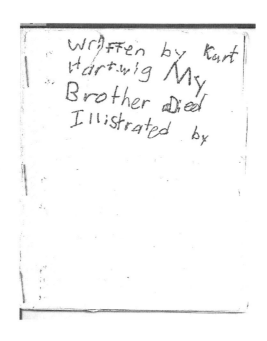

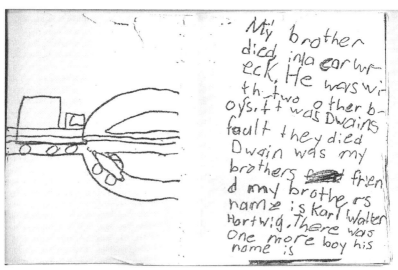

My friend is
Brace, he was
the first child
who knew about
it but he
didnt tell me
my parents
told me it was
Saturday when I
got the bad news.
I was troubled
all morning long.

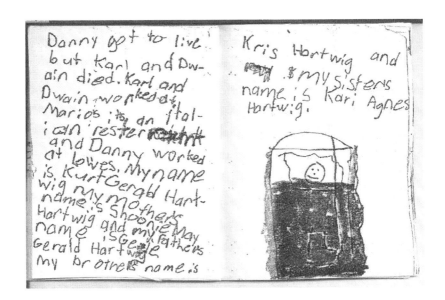

Danny got to live
but Karl and Dw-
ain died. Karl and
Dwain wonked at
Marios its an ital-
ian resteraunt
and Danny worked
at Lowes. My name
is Kurt Gerald Hart-
wig my mothers
name is Shoonie May
Hartwig and my fathers
name is Gerald Hartwig
my brothers name is

Kris Hartwig and
my & my sisters
name is Kari Agnes
Hartwig.

ABOUT THE
AUTHER Kurt
Hartwig is in
2cd grad I am
Kurt Hartwig its
very troublesom-
ne when someon
dies your family
book this is a true
book about my
nos I think you're brother and his

would have cried
to if Karl was
your brother
and he died I ho-
pe you do not
cry when you
read this book I
am very glad
to share this book
with you this book

Kurt knew about book writing from his dad, as his book was the topic of many family conversations. When Jerry completed the section "about the author", the kids were really impressed to see their names in print. Since Kurt started reading early, he began to pay attention to other book details. It's no surprise that he, too, included "about the author".

To write about this devastating loss, even at age seven was his attempt to make sense out of it all. His word world had already become a refuge. Maybe, just maybe, if he wrote about Karl's death, it would help him understand it.

We weren't the only ones trying to make some sense out of this seemingly meaningless death. During those first days of so many people coming to the house, one university friend looked at Jerry and me and asked, "How could this happen to you?"

Even in my beleaguered state, I knew that something very important had just been said. In all my growing up years with an absent father who died too young, I never heard my mother, Charlotte, ask, "Why?" or "What did we do to deserve this?" She continued to be about living, about creating, about loving, about running the race.

Even in my pillar, this remembering filtered into that frozen space. Several weeks later, on our way to church, Jerry and I were talking about this 'why' question. We were coming up a steep hill with a stop sign at the top. As Jerry shifted gears, I said with certainty, "The question is not 'why?'. The question is 'why not?'" We hovered in this first gear position for some time, pondering a new realization, one that we would return to over and over, again and again.

I resumed teaching piano at home and attending to the basics of family needs. To leave the house, to go out, anywhere but church, however, I simply couldn't do it. It was as if I had been stripped bare, with no protection. My flesh felt macerated.

Overexposure is terrifying. I knew sadness in my father's absence, but I didn't know any part of this excruciating, visceral, physical response that gouged my insides, that ripped apart my emotional stability, that shattered every pore of me so that the slightest touch, the merest glance shredded my skin as if I were on fire.

As this terrifying reality found excruciating living spaces within me,

---

there was another, equally terrifying possibility. The vulnerability of losing again became ever present. Karl was ripped out of our family with no warning.

It could happen again.

By December, my pillared space wasn't enough. I couldn't find escape anywhere. Within four months of living with this dreadful reality, I was being swallowed into an abyss of fear. Kristopher would be coming home for Christmas holidays, but Karl would never come home. Never again would he leave home. Never again would he return. The circularity of what he would not do and what we would not have ate away at me. Endings were everywhere.

I was suffocating inside my pillar.

When a church friend suggested I see a counselor at Duke hospital, I agreed. I knew that I couldn't be this person when Kristopher returned for the first time. I couldn't be this mother totally captured in Karl's absence, this mother whose whole being was grieving for this child. But I didn't know who else I could be.

The counselor, Wes Aitken, knew Kübler-Ross's stages of grief. It was small comfort to be named in denial. Nor was I interested in knowing which stages were ahead and how I would move from one to the next. During one session, Wes asked me to draw a circle representing my mother role and then from there, draw lines to each child. But after I drew the line to Karl, he took my pencil and scratched it out.

There was something in me that knew what he was trying to do. Get me to face reality. Get me to enter the present. I wanted to physically harm this man. All I remember is that I stood up and said, "I'm leaving."

Not a mother to Karl?

If he intended this to be shock therapy, I do not know, but it certainly had that effect. For the first time, I was forced to consider what all this might mean to my other children. They, too, were grieving and so was Karl's dad. Yet I didn't know who I was. I didn't know what kind of mother I was supposed to be now, or, what kind of wife.

The yellow tablet's words named me.

Yet in death we shut away our hearing ears and seeing eyes — our touching and caring — our growing — all our sources of creative being.

I was dead.

THERE IS HOPE FOR A TREE

How does a tree grow in the desert? How far down into the depths of the earth must the roots forge to seek moisture, life-giving nourishment amidst layers and layers of sand and heat? No light. Only dark upon dark. No sound. Only abyss upon abyss. I was a caked desert, parched, with no hint of blossoms.

How far down into the depths of the heart must the voice go before it can find a song to sing? I had become a sound vacuum. In church, others sang for me. The sanctuary of Abiding Savior held me yet I was mute.

Gradually, however, the piano became my wailing wall. The bench became my keening place. The timeless quality of music drew me into this distilling space where sound replaced any sense of before or after. Once the words started, they kept tumbling out with accompaniment following. Here is one.

The Courage to Be

I keep looking for a song to sing

I keep looking for the rainbow's ring

I keep looking for a face that I cannot see

Give me, O Lord, the courage to be

I keep waiting for my voice to sing

I keep waiting for the rainbow's ring

I keep waiting for a smile that I cannot see

Give me O Lord, the courage to be

When you hold out your hand

When you show me you care

My voice can sing out beyond its despair

Your spirit of love gives me strength to dare

To live once again though the ache in my heart

Engulfs me at times and sets me apart

For spirit is living though his face I cannot see

And spirit is loving

The Courage to be

Even though words and music wailed off the piano bench, they stayed on the musical score, silent, lifeless. Like the yellow tablet- *the courage to be-* named what was yet to be discovered.

Somehow, I lived as if on auto -pilot. There were times when I knew I had to dare leave the pillar but exhausting emotions blurred every day, every minute, every hour. I couldn't find myself. Then again, I wasn't really looking. Perhaps I was too afraid of what I'd find.

Several months after Karl's death, a woman called, introducing herself as one who shared with Jerry and me the experience of losing a child. She invited us to join an informal group in Chapel Hill named Compassionate Friends. She assured me that attending meetings brought no agenda other than a place to hear and if one chose, to speak about this shared reality.

In that gathering we discovered a new compassion not only for the suffering of others, but little by little, compassion for ourselves. The emotional space we were entering as a couple, however, was searingly difficult. All the 'what if', 'why', 'if only' questions spilled into this fearsome place of living without our son. Add to that, the emotions of anger, guilt, blame and you have a recipe for trouble.

When we learned that the divorce rate for parents after loss of a child is more than 90%, we were not surprised. With Karl's sudden death, there was no closure. Each of us had our very own relationship with him catapulting us into our own grieving pit where neither of us could support one another. We were alone yet inextricably bound together within this awful reality.

Only a few months later, we had a phone call from a church friend. "I know this is going to be very unusual," Barbara said, "but I have a request. You see, my sister Gloria's son committed suicide in her living room last week. She, along with two of her other children, witnessed it. I've heard that you and Jerry attend some kind of meetings with other parents whose children have died. Do you suppose you could take Gloria with you some time?"

"I don't know, Barbara," I replied. "First, it's hard to imagine that Gloria would really want to meet total strangers, including Jerry and me, when she is in such grief. And, the group in Chapel Hill, well, we're all white folk. Granted, we do share this awful reality of child loss, but would she really be comfortable in that setting?"

"Well," said Barbara, "I've told her about you, about Karl. She really wants to meet you, and I think if you would take her along with you to a meeting, then she could determine if she wants to continue."

We picked her up at her apartment in a public housing complex. From our first meeting, Jerry and I were struck with Gloria's profound human understanding. Among the several university and professional people in our Compassionate Friends group, she was the one who could most clearly articulate the turbulent emotions we were all experiencing. After she'd attended several meetings, she said, "It is so sad when mens can't cry."

About a year later, as we drove Gloria home, I told her that we wouldn't be going to the next meeting because our church was having a retreat in the mountains. "A retreat?" she asked. "What does that mean?" I explained a bit and she shook her head. "I've never heard of anything like that. Retreat."

Sometime later, I was talking with friend Rosa from church and told her about Gloria. She responded, "We should have a women's retreat. We could have several women from church and Gloria could bring her friends." It happened. Gloria invited five friends, all of whom worked with her at Duke University Hospital. Gloria was an elevator operator, and the others were employed in the laundry or kitchen. Now to figure out the essentials - car -pooling and food planning.

We arrived at Luther Rock late on a Saturday afternoon armed with fried chicken, biscuits, greens, and sweet potato pie for starters. The Duke group disappeared after a walkabout. No kids, no responsibilities? Time for a nap. When we gathered to eat and begin that getting-to-know-you process, not one woman in Gloria's group had ever had time out like this. Four of them were single parents; all of them had several dependent children as well as extended family members for whom they bore primary responsibility.

Linda, a social worker from church, suggested we try an exercise that she'd often used. She gave each of us a piece of paper. The instructions seemed straightforward. "Draw a circle like a pie," she said. "Now divide it into eight wedges. Think about each piece of the pie as ten years of your life. In each one, write down what you did, what you liked to do, what you wanted to do, the important people in your life. When you get to whatever is your present decade, write what you want to do in the future."

When we started going around the circle, describing each decade, I began to stand out. Significantly. Not only was I the only white woman present, I was the only one who repeatedly, decade after decade, spoke of creativity, whether singing, playing the piano or flute, reading or writing. I had chosen, very intentionally, to not name myself as a mother-of-a-son-who-died. Gloria knew and of course all my church friends. But to take this big step out of my pillar, it would strip me naked. Not yet.

The final question Linda asked us was to write in the last decade, what we hoped to do in the future. My response, "Grow old with my husband," caused astonishment from all gathered. And then, someone said, "We need to meet him!" followed by delighted laughter.

Several weeks later, Jerry was the male guest in our august female gathering. Before the evening ended, after considerable opportunities for him to respond to many questions, after telling of Karl's death, there was an affection born for this long-legged, casual, good man.

Over the next years, we moved on. I was hired at North Carolina Central University. I taught courses in African music, music education for primary school teachers, and theory/harmony as well as studio piano lessons. Jerry expanded his African research, taking him back to Sudan. Kristopher embarked on a pre-med course at St. Olaf. Kari was excited about applying to Earlham College. Kurt was Kurt.

What shook us loose from our ongoing sense of accustomed imbalance was a surprising call from St. Olaf College inviting Jerry to apply for the position of Vice-President, Academic Dean. It was early in 1980.

Might this be just the right place and time for Jerry to become an advocate for global perspectives in a liberal arts college? Leaving Durham, moving to a new community, might this be a positive change for each of us? For Kari, in particular, this possibility meant significant uprooting – her senior year in high school. But when the position was offered and all of us conferred, our decision was of one mind.

The pillar went with me, of course.

By late August, 1980, we were settling into a home in Northfield, Minnesota, into a house on the same street where I grew up. Jerry was discovering that his role as academic dean put him on the other side of the desk.

He left St. Olaf as a student. Now, in this new position, with a doctorate in African History, a former Duke Professor, a published scholar with significant global experience, he would be the mentor, a new voice advocating for an expanded curriculum, a teacher of teachers.

This is what he wrote to the search committee.

…What I could contribute to the St. Olaf community that would be distinctive is a conviction that diversity that is part of our world is a significant feature of God's creation. How we relate to diversity reflects on us as responsible Christians. It has been a feature of my life for two decades to examine and understand diversity, and it will continue to be important. As international and domestic tensions have demonstrated all too well, fear and hatred are comparatively easy to engender. Respect and love require more care, more nurturing.

The position seemed not only right, it seemed to be the right place, the right time. A new beginning.

Kristopher, as a senior, had been accepted for early admission to the University of North Carolina's medical school for the following year. Kari was braving the challenges of entering a senior high school class as a newcomer. Kurt, a fifth grader, was fine as long as he had armfuls of library books.

Since I left my piano and university teaching behind, it made sense that I take a year to get my bearings. There was so much to take in, settling into these old-and-new communities of Northfield and St. Olaf, our kids in their new settings and my own mother, now eighty-four, living only a few blocks away.

A job could wait. Not only had we left Karl-memory-places, we left a cultural environment of diversity in our work, community and church. Now we were in Minnesota white, everywhere.

In late September, Jerry was invited to address the St. Olaf community during a Chapel service. His application letter for consideration as Dean of the College was now being translated into his vision of what the college could become.

I want to discuss community with you today because there is a desire on the part of some students, some administrators, some faculty and myself to increase the minority presence on this campus. But I would ask for serious reflection on the motives behind such a desire, the sincerity of that wish, and whether the necessary energy will, and commitment is present to incorporate others.

Do we dare to invite Martin Luther King, Jr.'s dream into our vision for the St. Olaf community? Do we dare to be open to the bond of God's love that goes beyond our homogeneous niche?

Are we we ready

- *To listen – as well as to talk*

- *To learn – as well as to teach*

- *To receive – as well as to give*

- *To love – so that we may gain?*

A man with a vision.

October in the Midwest. Sunday, the 19th. We reveled in the autumnal colors, the scrunch of leaves underfoot when walking our dog, Simba, our fireplace ablaze for nighttime reading. It was the season of pumpkins. A carving candidate for Kurt came in the arms of a retired member of the biology department that afternoon.

It had been a splendid day. We had attended church at St. John's, returning home to tune into the campus service as the intern, Kristine Carlson, was preaching. Jerry didn't want to miss it. Besides, the Ole choir was singing. Kristopher and his cousin Jeff, tenor and bass, joined us for lunch.

During our conversation, Jerry asked, "What did you think about the sermon topic of serendipity?"

Although he was the one who asked the question, it became clear as we talked about the many aspects of this unusual word – providence, chance, destiny – that this beloved husband of mine was close to tears. This unplanned, unanticipated community we had entered seemed to overflow

71

with possibilities. For the past three years, we had come to a new awareness of living and dying. Perhaps, just perhaps, in this new place, our desert might begin to blossom.

At suppertime, given the chill in the air, we decided to light a fire. Kari gathered her homework, settling into the cozy armchair. Jerry, with a glass of wine and an article to review for an African History journal, settled into his great- grandfather's rocking chair. I was upstairs at my desk when the phone rang. Dear friends from North Carolina were calling to check in.

Suddenly, in the midst of our conversation, I heard a terrifying yell from Kari, "MOM! MOM!"

Running downstairs, Kari was hovering over her dad who was slumped in the rocker, motionless. Her voice quavering, she said, "I just asked him a question about my homework and when he didn't answer…oh mom, what is happening?"

Time froze. Somehow I call 911. I deliver mouth-to-mouth resuscitation. Paramedics usher Kurt, Kari and me into the kitchen. We can hear them. We stand speechless, transfixed. We hear the counting voices through the door as they administer electric shock. When the door opens, a man says, "We're taking him to the hospital in the ambulance. Someone will bring all of you by car."

Our yard is full of neighbors responding to the omen of a siren. Jerry, on a gurney, is put into the ambulance. We stumble into a car, following.

Kristopher, summoned from campus, joins us. We hold on to one another, not daring to speak. Long minutes, unending, we wait. A doctor comes with the words, "I'm so sorry. He suffered a massive heart attack, and all measures to restore his life have failed."

The words cannot be taken in. It all happened too quickly. There is no comprehension. It is as if we have entered a surreal time warp.

We are ushered into a sterile room. We circle this bed where there is a motionless form. It's impossible to comprehend. We can't move. It can't be. This husband, this father is lifeless. Somehow, we kiss his forehead, hold his hand. And then sobbing of disbelief erupts. We don't want to leave. We can't walk out the door. If we do, we leave him behind. It is too terrifying. Desperately, we hold on to one another.

Home. Home without. Now we are four. Kristopher offers to make the first phone calls to immediate family and North Carolina friends. Kari helps with the list. I am rooted to the couch in the living room. People, family, friends are filing in and out.

When our doctor neighbor sits next to me, hours into the night, his question is overwhelming to my numbed state. "I'm really sorry to ask you this, but the mortician needs to know your answer before morning. Will you want cremation or a burial for Jerry?"

In some remote consciousness within me, I knew what we must do. The summer of Karl's death, Karl told me about seeing an eagle, stunning and majestic as it soared. "I wish I could do that!" he'd said. Somehow, our conversation continued to dying, perhaps because of his grandmother's illness causing him to write that letter.

And then, he said, very quietly, "I want to be cremated."

If we had not had that conversation, it's hard for me to imagine that we would have chosen cremation. It was new to everyone in our family. We spread Karl's ashes in a beautiful canopied space in Duke Forest, near one of his favorite fishing streams. Sometime later, Jerry and I agreed that we, too, would want the same when it was our time, the same process, the same place.

But now, it no longer felt right. Everything had changed. My primary thought was for Jerry's parents, Faith and Walt. Karl's cremation had been difficult for them. They knew the traditional embalming, casket and cemetery burial, not ashes in a wooded glen with no marker. Even though Jerry had expressed his wish, somehow I knew that it would be very difficult for them to accept this very different process for their only son.

Other questions were already surfacing in those first hours. Kurt looked at me soon after our return from the hospital and said, "I need to get a paper route."

Kristopher said, "I'm moving home."

They were way ahead of me.

And then there was Kari, back in her role of answering telephone calls, doorbells, hosting. Not surprisingly, one evening she said very quietly, "I really don't want to do this again!"

Later, crawling into bed with me, I grabbed her hand and asked, "What's going to happen to us?"

Teetering on the brink. All of us. The familiarity of what had to be done those first days somehow propelled us forward. Family gathered along with so many from Abiding Savior and Duke. In the midst was Charlotte, organizing, helping, still running the race. Kristopher and my brother Gus chose a burial site in Northfield's Oaklawn cemetery.

As preparations for Jerry's memorial service began, there were some inclusions that were certain. St. Olaf's president, Harlan Foss gave the eulogy based on the Old Testament prophet Micah's response to the question, "What does the Lord require of you? Do justice, love kindness and walk humbly with your God." This Jerry knew and lived.

My yellow tablet response to, "What is it to live and to die?" was folded into his pants pocket, always. Kristine Carlson, whose serendipity sermon touched Jerry so deeply, would read it.

Before the service began in Boe Chapel on the St. Olaf campus, we gathered, waiting for the signal to enter the sanctuary. Many of our Durham friends were in the mix. When the funeral director stepped forward, looking at all of us, clearly of varying hues, to declare, "Now is the time for only family to enter," my eyes and my heart looked at this amazingly beautiful collective of God's creation and I said, "This IS our family!"

At this point, Kurt took my hand, looking up at me with all the seriousness of a ten-year old, he asked, "Are you going to get married again?"

Forty-five years. That was Jerry's life span. Twenty-two years, our marriage. We had moved to Northfield with the possibilities of what his work might yield at St. Olaf. Standing at the gravesite, we buried his body. That his spirit might live, somehow in the depths of my soul, I believed in the possibility. I had written words about spirit living but only began learning what might be required to live that knowing after Karl's death. Now we were all on a new path with no sense of direction.

During his brief six weeks as Dean of the College, Jerry had had occasion to meet with many faculty. Most surprising was the interest he had engendered within the student body. The editorial staff of the student weekly, *The Manitou Messenger*, interviewed him, questioning him about his background with particular interest about his international research. Photographers were busily snapping pictures during their conversations. Later, the kids and I would pore over each one, wondering, "Now what do you think they just asked him?"

The week after Jerry's death, there was a full back page picture of autumn in the wooded slopes behind the campus.

At the bottom, this inscription from the book of Job: "For there is hope for a tree if it is cut down that it will sprout again and its roots shall not cease."

It wasn't just the sensitivity of students' response to the sudden death of this newcomer to campus.

The picture.

It is exactly like Karl's place in Duke Forest.

THE RINGS

When we left our home of ten years on Rolling Hill Road in Durham, we left without Karl. When we returned from the hospital to our home of only six weeks on Manitou street in Northfield, we entered without Jerry – three fatherless children with a husband-less mother.

The 'without' factor was more than naming, it was another wrenching life changing reality for each of us. Heart sore from Karl's death only three years earlier, our grief quotient was over flowing. Now this new shattering, sudden departure of a father and husband left each of us desperately wondering how we'd survive.

A family pillar. The four of us intuited our overwhelming need to be present with one another. This was not a time of rational thinking; only emotional realities reigned. Might we find some stability in our quaking selves if we began and ended each day together? When each of us walked out our front door, we faced daunting challenges. It was a blessed assurance to know that we would return to our family unit every evening.

It started with Kristopher's decision to move home. It made all the difference. He brought a daily balm to each of us with his steady, gentle, humoring presence. During the day, he re-entered his normal world of classes, choir, cousins and friends, bringing us anecdotes at night. Often, friends accompanied him to join our supper table. He also knew where he was going after graduation. Early admittance to the University of North Carolina's medical school meant a fall return to a region with which he was already familiar.

Kari, unlike her older brother, had started out as a senior-new-comer to the Northfield high school scene. Not an enviable position for anyone, particularly a teenage girl. Now, six weeks later, she suddenly became the senior whose father died, not an easy entre to well- established friend cliques.

She had no one to invite home, no group with whom to hang out. We were it. Furthermore, she didn't know where she was going after her graduation in May. We had stopped at Earlham College on our drive from North Carolina to Minnesota. It seemed like just the right place for her with its global and social service ethic. But now, nothing was certain.

Then there was fifth grader, Kurt, whose response to his newcomer status began to show a pattern, but it took me a while to get it.

The first evidence occurred in January, about three months after his dad's death. He complained of not feeling well enough to go to school, although the ritual testing with a thermometer showed no fever. Nonetheless, his lethargy was such that I agreed to a day at home.

The month of January at St. Olaf offers only one course of study. Thinking that it would push me out of the house to study C.S. Lewis with Professor Bill Narum, I left for class with Kurt's agreement.

Upon my return, I noticed that the phone book was open on the kitchen counter. Looking at Kurt with some puzzlement, I asked, "Have you been calling anyone?"

"Yup. I called Bea Foss."

"You called BEA FOSS," I exclaimed – as in – wife of St. Olaf's President living four doors away.

"I needed you," was his matter of fact reply. "I knew she could find you."

Gradually, it became apparent that for him to leave home for school or for any other reason was problematic. He could handle school but only for a few weeks at a time. At first, I relented, but as the pattern became more obvious, I'd even drive him to school hoping that it would help. It didn't.

Finally, we made a deal. Every six weeks, he had a free day at home, no fever, no anything, just a day at home. It made all the difference, as gradually, he could leave and survive the outside exposure.

Pillars come in all sizes.

That left me, trying to go out the door. The propulsion to move me could be summarized in one word: survival. With Jerry's death, I was responsible not only for the kids' well being but for our financial survival. I was startlingly without, which is the dictionary definition of *widow*.

The kids and I came to an agreement to stay in Northfield. We simply couldn't imagine the four of us returning to Durham. This meant that I would need to find employment in Northfield. It also meant that I was now responsible for two homes as our house had yet to sell on Rolling Hill Road. Furthermore, there was no assurance that St. Olaf would continue Kristopher's aid package. This all translated to a living nightmare.

Even in my beleaguered state, it was clear that Northfield already had more than enough musicians. Although I had a master's degree in music, it wasn't evident to me that I could significantly contribute within this milieu. Over the next weeks and months, the kids and I began to talk about what credentials I had that might be of interest.

Meanwhile, the immediate concerns were for the Durham house, which finally sold in April. A month after Jerry's death, St. Olaf notified me that Kristopher's financial aid package would cease. Miraculously, I received a letter in early December from a Duke official that the University would cover all of his second semester expenses. Kari's hopes for Earlham would not be possible.

Gradually, conversations at our kitchen table expanded to several St. Olaf faculty and administrators. Jerry's vision of expanding a global awareness at the college became my focus. Our Tanzania and North Carolina experiences became the framework for a job description that I submitted to President Foss in March 1981. It looked like this:

Intercultural Liaison (part-time): To facilitate new academic programs expanding possibilities for students' study within and outside the US to further their global awareness; to be a global advocate through student groups – multicultural/international.

St. Olaf accepted the proposal; I began my new position in September 1981. My initial focus was to develop 'The Durham Connection' as a January course offering. It would be centered with our Abiding Savior families who would offer home stays to students. Faculties at Duke, UNC/Chapel Hill, North Carolina Central University, community and health organizations would be primary resources for student inquiry on the African American experience.

I also began exploring possibilities of developing a student study abroad- exchange program between the University of Dar es Salaam, Tanzania and selected ELCA colleges. At this time, in the early '80s, very few programs were established in Africa; we were breaking new ground.

Before our move from North Carolina to Minnesota, Jerry and I had talked with Kristopher, Kari, and Kurt about a trip back to Tanzania. For Kristopher, heading to med school with global intent, Kari a senior in high school with a service learning leaning and Kurt who had never been to Africa, it seemed the right time to re-affirm who we were as a family and to do so in this place that had shaped us so significantly.

But to go without Jerry, for me, seemed impossible. Yet the kids were of a mind; we needed to make this trip. For Kristopher and Kari, it would be a return to not only remember place and friends, it held the possibility of shaping their future decisions. And for Kurt, who had only known Tanzania through story, he wanted to see it with his own eyes. As a new family of four, we had become very aware of how each of us walked out the door every morning and re-entered every evening. I trusted their judgment.

With my new position beginning in the fall, a Tanzania return would be more than reconnecting with friends. Now I had a new focus for I would meet with officials at the University of Dar es Salaam to discuss the possibilities of an exchange program.

During our Arusha visits, we stayed with two families, the Simonsons and the Bensons, friends from our earliest days at Ilboru Secondary School. In the mix, Rebecca Smith joined us. She had spent her first seven years with her missionary parents in Moshi. Now she was investigating possible work opportunities after completing her nursing degree. Her gentle presence and guitar strumming drew Kurt to her side. Then there was Kristopher who met, saw and committed. They married two years later.

After those remarkable weeks, Kurt and I returned home alone. Kristopher started medical school in Chapel Hill, and Kari moved on campus at St. Olaf as a first-year student. For the past ten months, we had all been under the same roof, a blessed time of presence to one another. Now, each of us faced our own new beginnings.

Responsible is a very thick word. Its revelations in my new widow status seemed to bring daily discoveries. With Charlotte only blocks away, it became evident over the next years that she, too, would need more support from me. Mostly, I tried to ignore this reality.

When we moved to Northfield, she'd retired after twenty-three years of teaching piano at St. Olaf. However, Carleton College hired her immediately as a part-time teacher. For five years, until she was eighty, she sometimes walked across town from her apartment, or if weather required, called a taxi.

If there was a Widow Woman Extraordinaire, it was Charlotte. As a full-time, working mom, her life-style was my norm. Growing up with her was one thing. But now I was seeing her with a new awareness, not only as her daughter but now as a widow. It would take me a while to grasp the significant similarities between us. Between my new job and single parenting, I was focused on my own survival. But inevitably, I began to wonder how she did it all.

Meanwhile, the job as Intercultural Liaison was giving me a new focus. Within a year, the foundation for the Durham Connection was laid so that in January 1982, I was driving two Olaf students to Durham. Kurt resided in the back of the rental station wagon. He stayed with his best friend, Bruce White on Rolling Hill Road. During the day, sometimes he went with Bruce to his old primary school in Hope Valley. For two years, this worked, but the third year, his cousin, Gregg Ramseth, who was working at St. Olaf, came to our house every night.

Over the next four years, meetings continued with representatives from several ELCA colleges to explore the exchange program possibilities at the University of Dar es Salaam. A key component in its development centered on the exchange aspect that would offer students from both continents opportunities for a global experience. This was not the norm for study abroad programs, but I held on to this critical tenet.

Two years into our discussions, the University of Dar es Salaam threw us a curve ball. Instead of students, they wanted faculty in the exchange, those who needed access to libraries and internet, whether for their doctoral literature reviews or for research and subsequent publications.

This meant that different housing would be required for Tanzanian faculty. In addition, the exchange required ELCA students to live in university – student housing. The accompanying ELCA faculty person would travel with them, but after two weeks of orientation, the students were on their own, attending classes, living, eating and learning like all other international students.

In July of 1985, we were ready to launch the Lutheran College Consortium with Tanzania. I accompanied four stalwart ELCA students to Dar es Salaam. During my absence, Kurt was farmed out to relatives – primarily Jerry's sister and husband, Jackie and Jerry Hanson. Perhaps you are seeing an historical pattern here. Not me. I was too busy trying to balance my responsibilities between family and job.

Survival ruled. Yet the pillar also was becoming a seeding place for new beginnings. Scary. It was all so new, new in my associations, new in program development, new in my solo role. My voice was changing everywhere.

On campus, there were other developments finding programmatic footing. 'Zebra Patch' became a new incarnation of 'Are You Listening?' The difference was to expand the African and African American literary and musical expressions to a broader global representation including Asian, Hispanic, Native American voices. I also initiated 'Roundtable' gatherings of students, faculty and administrators for Sunday afternoon coffee or tea to exchange ideas around a global topic.

The connections between who I had been, where I had been and who I was becoming in this new setting were feeding my creative spirit. Drawing on our Tanzania and North Carolina experiences, a wealth of friends and colleagues encouraged, supported and walked with me. This included very especially, each of my three kids, every step of the way. They carried their dad's spirit.

Jerry's passion for African history transcended the academic setting. As a family, our sense of belonging included his commitment to what would be required of us in our global world. This intersecting vision within our household challenged us to 'hear the beat from the far off shore and the beat right next door'. It was this vision that fed my programmatic and teaching evolvement. A new sense of vocation was emerging.

...the eternal spirit can spring to life if there is someone who can love us enough that we dare risk life once again...

Resurrecting imagination isn't easy. On the one hand, you could say that this is the essence of living. But walking on water? If my kids' imaginations hadn't been kindled, if Jerry hadn't supported me in my own creative ventures, I wouldn't have had the courage to dare. What I would discover was that there would be others, others who had no history with me, but their imaginations were drawn to the new beat.

Not surprisingly, I carried a singular identity marker at St. Olaf: widow of a dean who died from a heart attack. Although Jerry's tenure was short, he had already made a significant impression. His global experience and academic stature was matched with his sense of service and justice. My association with his legacy was apparent in meetings where, as a newcomer, I was generously welcomed. Gradually, I began to discover my new voice, emerging from my pillar.

Within four years, I was invited to develop an introductory course for a new curriculum offering – American Racial Minority Studies – and a senior seminar in Women's Studies on Cross- Cultural Women. Two faculty members, in particular, mentored me in this process – Connie Gengebach and Jim Farrell. Their advice, counsel and encouragement made all the difference.

Connie had a two -department affiliation – Religion and History and Jim - American Studies. As we were on a curriculum committee together, they encouraged me to enter the teaching realm even without proper credentials. Without their advocacy, I'd never have imagined it, never mind considered it as a possibility.

At one meeting, I made this comment, "We've been carefully taught by what we've not been taught". Jim asked me later if he could quote me in his book. He did. But he also counseled me about pulling back, just a bit, with my cross-cultural passionate voice. Imagine!

Connie developed cancer three years later. At one of our Zebra Patch presentations, a student read "What is it to live and to die?" Connie came up to me afterwards and asked for a copy. At that time, I had no idea that her life was precarious.

She died within that year. In the planning of her service, Connie asked if I would read her scripture selections indicating that I should feel free to change any gendered language. I walked many blocks after her husband's call.

My North Carolina-Abiding Savior family collaborated and supported me in the Durham Connection. Without Rosa Small teaming with me, members of our congregation opening up their homes, neighbors Ludie and Fred White and Linde Wittmann hosting me, John Hope Franklin and many members of UNC and Duke faculty mentoring me – I couldn't have done it.

Then there were the Tanzanian connections supporting me from Simonson and Benson households to Justin Maeda, Keto and Grace Mshigeni at the University of Dar es Salaam. The concepts of exchange and partnership, of reciprocity and shared responsibility were seeding.

Authority. Who has it? Whose voice carries it? What spaces proclaim it? These are extraordinarily treacherous waters to navigate particularly as a white female whether in the U.S. or Tanzania. My learning curve challenged me at every turn whether in the classroom, negotiating partnered programs, in mediation consults, in chosen texts for study, in church. Everywhere.

Throughout these survival - responsible early years as Intercultural Liaison, I began to realize a new self-awareness signaled by the authority of my wedding rings. One evening, just before turning off the bedside lamp, my left hand caught my attention. 'This isn't me anymore,' was in my head. I was only a three -year old widow, yet my identity had been irrevocably changed. Slowly, I took both rings off, putting them by the lamp. My hand was bereft, naked even. In the morning, I quickly put them back on. The idea was in my head but not my heart.

It wasn't as if anyone was telling me to do this. Charlotte, widowed forty-five years at that point, had never taken her rings off. Like widows of her generation, they were there to stay unless they remarried. Women in my age group signaled divorce or dating when they removed their rings. For me, it was my personal symbolic process of identity discovery.

If I took the rings off, I acknowledged that without Jerry's living presence, I was no longer married. This didn't mean I negated our twenty-two years together. But it did mean that what I had known in the past in our relationship was being transformed. And somehow, the rings were the primary symbols of this process.

The next time I took them off, they remained off. My weightless fourth finger screamed for attention. So, one morning, I walked, probably marched into the kitchen, put my hands out in front of Kurt who was trying to eat his cereal and announced, "What do you see?" A bit confused, he looked at me with a puzzled expression and said, "Your hands?"

"There are no rings on my left hand!" I exclaimed.

As if this was the most ordinary news, Kurt looked at me through his thick glasses and said quite matter-of-factly, "Well, Mom, he's not coming back you know."

No frills or embellishments. As I gradually became acquainted with my ring loss, I was also aware of others in the family who might not respond like Kurt. Because Kristopher, Kari and Kurt were such a part of all the changes evolving, they understood.

It was not easy for Jerry's folks who found the removing of my rings problematic. Only a week after his death, Faith had asked me to please not remarry for at least a year. Her fear that her son would be displaced was acute. Within a year, each of the kids received a beautiful picture album chronicling their dad's life with special attention paid to each of them.

My ring explanation simply made no sense to them. If I wasn't dating, why was this necessary? Trying to explain how all these new experiences in Northfield, St. Olaf and as a single parent were giving me a new self-awareness didn't seem to help. But the rings stayed off.

I couldn't go back. I couldn't go back to being Jerry's wife. By removing my rings, I acknowledged this reality. I needed to make my way forward. The absence of his physical presence, however, could not, would not deny his spiritual presence. Yet, I was on a solo journey, living between absence and presence. It's a difficult tune to learn.

The rings, like me, were in transformation. The diamond and wedding band signified my identity as a married woman. This would change. The gold was melted and reshaped. A local goldsmith designed a pendant with my engagement diamond surrounded by four gold balls representing each of our kids. Throughout our twenty-two years of marriage, we discovered together new worlds of people and place. We had a shared centerpiece in our evolving world-view, in our research, in our life commitments, in our faith. We knew a delight of presence. This memory reality could not be changed by ring transformation.

Nor did it change my aching heart. All of me mourned. Once again, the piano bench became my keening place. The words of "I Call You By Name" paraphrase Isaiah's writing and African theologian John Mbiti's words:

I Call You By Name

The seed of love, it has been sown

You are my child

You are my own

I call you by name

It has been, it is, it will always be the same,

Wherever you are

I call you by name.

Child, child, who goes before,

Child who is right now

Child, child who is yet to be

Fear not, I call you by name

The accompanying music is a four part choral setting, written in 5/4 time, symbolizing the unevenness in living between fear and security, despair and hope, living and dying. Yet the knowing of being called by name, seemingly hidden, *is*. There are two solos, one for tenor and one for bass. When brother-in-law Jerry Hanson performed it with his choir at First Lutheran in Sioux Falls, South Dakota, Kristopher and his cousin, Jeff, Jackie and Jerry's son, were the soloists.

At the bottom of the score, I wrote this:

"Through life's unevenness and life's inequities, God calls our name and stills our fears. For it is this love that covers us all – in all times – in all places.

And so, too, we can dare to love.

For my Jerry who was, is and will always be my love."

PRACTICING

The piano bench became my first teacher in understanding what it means to practice. Presumably, it is the repetition that makes the difference. I learned to isolate sections of a composition that were most difficult. First, this meant finger training, starting slowly so as to become accustomed to the configurations. Then, gradually, I'd fit the sections back into the whole composition, a prelude to discovering the music's heart and soul.

I found this part of practicing totally boring. I wanted to skip all that repeating, and just get to the entire piece. But if I did that, without paying attention to difficult passages, inevitably, my fingers balked. Furthermore, without this painstaking, careful preparation, the notes remained notes. The composition waited to become music.

Survival practicing exercises can be numbing. Without knowing it, I was going through the motions without any sense of the compositional whole. Reflective awareness would come twenty-three years later when I began to write poetry.

'Practicing Resurrection ', hints at these myriad pieces that over the many years of phase repetitions, continued.

PRACTICING RESURRECTION

Too many flats

Beat unfathomable

Largo absurdum

Time

Standing

Still

Alleluias

Stuck

In

My

Throat

Lent eternal

Bach

B minor

Sunday

Hymns

Others sing

Others speak

Mute

First verses

Living with absence

Sleepless

Numbing

Heartbreak

   Darkness

Overwhelming

Second verses

  Aorta dissecting

     Heart wailing

Third verses

   Soul sustenance bereft

BURY ME

Fourth verses

   Silence

   Deafening

   Abject fear

       You Still Have a Race to Run

  Ears tune out

    You Still Have a Race to Run

   A faint melody

Voices singing in silence

    A Race to Run?

  A hum

Can be generative

  A grief

   Transposing

A race to run. Charlotte's words hours after Karl's death stayed with me. She was not a frequent Bible quoting woman, but this Hebrews verse she'd paraphrase at particular times when perseverance might cause her kids to stumble.

Hebrews 12:1 "As for us, we have this large crowd of witnesses around us…so let us run with determination the race that lies before us…let us keep our eyes on Jesus."

It was about four years after Jerry's death when I suddenly realized that I had been practicing Charlotte's five-finger *Running the Race Exercises*: faith, family, education, service and creative perseverance. Several months ago, I attended the wedding of Karen Audrey Donhowe, my brother Jack's granddaughter. As I had just framed this exercise, I tried it out with several of her uncles. There was this look of astonishment in the naming, their heads slowly nodding and then, "That's it! That's Gaum (their naming of their grandmother) and that's us!"

This awareness came to me as I was writing this 'Practicing' section. Needless to say, there are many variations on the themes within the five- finger exercise. Between higher education degrees and creative perseverance, we are an interesting family. Musicians, artists, doctors, writers, preachers and teachers, to name a few, are born from daring to imagine again, to bring to life possibilities in a new key.

As her daughter, I knew a mom dedicated to work and to her kids. That she was a widow, I knew from observation. It was a role I consciously acknowledged to be too overwhelmingly difficult, hoping that I'd never know it.

Now, I was beginning to see her with new eyes and heart. I was beginning to understand how her unswerving belief in the *large crowd of witnesses*, and *keeping her eyes on Jesus* had sustained her. Her vocation was more than piano teaching; it was how she taught, how she lived.

Charlotte was known as the walker. Her purposeful stride each morning towards St. Olaf and her piano studio was only deterred with torrents of rain, ice or snow. Her assumption of God presence was not relegated to her role as a mother. Rather, it permeated her professional and relational world.

Her belief was grounded in a grace filled Jesus whose living knew suffering yet God's promise of unfailing love and forgiveness at the core of life. She was not playing a solo; she was joining a chorus of multitudes who already knew the score. I grew up observing how she translated this day by day.

Charlotte was a no nonsense mother and teacher, not particularly endowed with great humor though she could enjoy others. She was very serious about running the race, doing your best. She could have written a best seller: "Practicing Resurrection for Dummies", but as I write this, I know she wouldn't find my humor very amusing.

In my early years of widowhood, I was too busy surviving to see our astonishing life parallels. My gradual awareness is best understood this way.

Charlotte's mother died suddenly when she was three years old.

She grew up in a motherless household.

My Dad died suddenly just before I turned three.

I grew up in a fatherless household.

Charlotte's husband died suddenly at the age of forty-four.

She became a widow with five children.

My husband died suddenly at the age of forty-five.

I became a widow with three children.

Charlotte moved to Northfield so that she could teach at St. Olaf.

She was forty-four.

I was newly moved to Northfield and would teach at St. Olaf.

I was forty-five.

It is stunning in its revelation. As I read this, written on the page, it seems so obvious. So why did it take so long for me to get it? Perhaps it was because I was too busy trying to live, trying to survive. The chronology parallel simply didn't register. When it did, an amazement and wonder overwhelmed me because I began to realize that I was living two lives – my

own – and my mom's. This was as disquieting as it was disturbing.

It's no surprise that I also knew that I would need to write

Charlotte's memoir. The title came quickly - *A Sonata for Four Hands*. It

would be her story with her hands on the keyboard, her score, her

composition. I would be the writer, her page- turner. Not unlike my

youngest when he wrote after Karl's death, perhaps this would guide me in

my years waiting to be lived.

She would be ninety-years old before I would begin. Her long life

span provided an invaluable perspective for the writing. I began to see how

her five finger exercises translated into a full, well-lived life for she never

lost her sense of where she was going or who was going with her.

Yet I was living in the initial practicing stage. I suffered from an

attention deficit. I could focus on fragments, but I couldn't imagine the

compositional whole. I didn't have a name for it. I only knew I was heart

sore and weary, so much so, that at times, I couldn't put my fingers to the

keyboard.

And yet even in my pillar, there was always a trace of a hum.

Sometimes, hearing 'it is well with my soul', at church, or Kristopher calling

to announce the arrival of my first grandchild, Jenny Rebekah, or Kari,

joining two busloads of St. Olaf students for the march on Washington, or

Kurt's first theatrical role at age twelve – one line in the first and one in the second act– looking for me in the audience for every one of fourteen performances.

Resurrection. For each one of us there were new beginnings filled with life. A young family with a newborn, a civil rights march, a story acted out on stage - were giving each one a new sense of possibility and life meaning. They weren't alone.

Between my kids, teaching, starting a January Term in Durham, North Carolina, facilitating the foundation for the exchange program in Tanzania and assisting Charlotte, my practicing was fragmented. Too many phrases. The verses kept repeating with a relentless ferocity. Where was the hum?

My vulnerability in all my responsible roles sometimes roared over me with a tsunami force. One morning I awakened with a dream so vivid, I didn't need an interpreter.

I was walking up St. Olaf Avenue from home to my office on campus. As I began climbing the many steps up the hill, suddenly, I was totally naked, not a stitch of clothing. It gave new meaning to my continuing understanding of being *without*.

I ran for cover but the Norway pines offered no refuge. Desperately, I looked around only to see that students were leaving Old Main, the sidewalk and street congested as they ambled to their next classes. There was no hiding place.

To get to my office, I would have to join the throng. If I'd grown up in Sweden, such a dream would probably have been an opportunity rather than a threat. But I grew up in a single parent household in Northfield- with modest Charlotte. No more need be said.

The dream was too real. The incessant demands in my many roles had voices well beyond a hum; they could become a roar. If only I could put my rings back on; if only Jerry and Karl hadn't died; if only my life wasn't congested with so much absence. If only.

This included Charlotte. If only her aging didn't require more of my attention. Living in the same community, seeing her almost daily, I failed to notice changes. When we moved to Northfield, she was eighty-four. When she was retired from St. Olaf at age seventy, Carleton's music department hired her immediately. Even though she was part-time, her days had a bench focus.

When she stopped teaching at age eighty-five, this seemed to trigger changes. My brother Gus was the first to name it. Living in St. Paul, he and his wife, Ruth, would come to Northfield about every six weeks. They began to notice her increasing frailty and that she paid less attention to her appearance.

Between Perman's Clothing Store in downtown Northfield, and Dayton's in Minneapolis, her wardrobe was small but well chosen. She had a good eye for color and design. As a professional woman, her attire completed an aura of dignity with a modest flair. Her hair, barely streaked with grey, she braided into a French coronet. The result, one classy lady.

When Gus first voiced his concerns for Charlotte's independent well being, I have to admit that it really, really made me angry. But then, I, too, began to notice changes in her attention to details – like wearing the same dresses over and over or forgetting to pay bills.

Gus suggested that he broach the subject of a move to assisted living within the Northfield Retirement Center complex. For Charlotte, any suggestion coming from son Gus was not only heard but seriously considered. He had an amazing ability to speak of important matters, book ended with humor and laughter. She agreed with no questions or concerns. She trusted his judgment completely.

Prior to the move required going through all of her possessions and determining what she could take with her and what family wanted. Peg came to stay for a week to help mom sort through it all. And then a discovery in the attic that made all the difference. It was a small box containing all the letters exchanged between my mom and dad before they were married.

Letters written from Story City to Denver. None of us had ever seen them. I had never seen my dad's hand-writing. We were all enthralled, reading several daily to the great joy of everyone. We were all transported back to that wonderful time of everything still possible, still waiting to be discovered.

Mom would listen as the letters were read with a sense of contentment, for without a doubt, the relating of events they were living at that time, of the love so beautifully expressed between the two of them, brought her comfort as she faced one more challenge. This move ended her independent living, her teaching, her hosting, everything she had done to give life meaning. It meant leaving the piano bench. She was eighty-seven.

When her neighbor friend, who had lived in her home for more than fifty years, asked, "Charlotte, how is it possible for you to do this?" it is not surprising that she said "I've done many things more difficult than this." Yet, she spoke in past tense. What she couldn't have imagined was yet to come only a year later.

It was a bitter cold that 16th day of December in 1984. Classes were over. I was preparing for Christmas with Kristopher, Rebecca and their daughter Jenny joining us. Suddenly, a St. Olaf friend burst into the house and said, "Oh Shoonie, it's Betty Ann." Only those words, and I knew. I knew this beloved sister was no longer among the living.

The particulars, the question, 'what happened?' I couldn't ask. I couldn't ask because the only thought I had was, "How, HOW can I possibly tell Mom?"

When Gus and I entered her room in the Retirement Center, Charlotte's face lit up immediately sighting the two of us. But then, as she began to absorb this news, her diminishing eighty-eighty-year-old body began to tremble. Her tears fell silently and I thought, "Is this another aging phenomenon, or is her heart and soul so sorrow filled, she can't absorb any more?"

We celebrated Betty Ann's sixty-four years in her Sacramento church community as well as in Northfield. This wife, mother and musician brought many near and far to celebrate her creative and loving life. As our family gathered to mourn, our collective memories of accumulating absences continued to multiply.

Peg without Jule

Jack without Audrey

Me without Jerry and Karl

Rudy without Betty Ann

Each time we gathered, we sang, "For All the Saints." But for too many of Charlotte's grandchildren, the spiritual, "Sometimes I feel like a motherless/fatherless child" was becoming too familiar. With Betty Ann's death, we were also mourning Jule, Jerry, Karl and Audrey.

As for me, once again I retreated – mute - into my pillar. Not even a hum. By now, I had significant acquaintance with this space. There was no choice. I just went there; it was not a conscious decision. But now, as I write this, and in reflection over these many years, I realize that part of me died each time.

Yet I couldn't stay there for long. Survival practicing required my attention. As an Intercultural Liaison, I was learning. I was the student whether facilitating new off- campus programs in North Carolina and Tanzania or teaching 'American Racial and Minority Studies' or 'Women's Studies' in the classroom.

In addition, I had been asked to assist in the development of sexual harassment policies, to initiate a mediation program as well as to support emerging student populations who felt they were outsiders. I needed a 'Teach Yourself' book for I'd had no formal education to prepare me for what I was doing.

By 1991, I'd been discovering myself for eleven years since Jerry's death. Our kids were doing the same. Kristopher and Rebecca had a family of four – Daniel, Jenny, Kirsten and Heidi – Nate Seth was born two years later. They were living on the shores of Lake Victoria in Shirati, Tanzania where Kristopher worked in a Mennonite hospital. Returning to the States in '94, he joined a family practice in Westfield, New York. When an opening for Hospice Care came to their attention, Kristopher nodded.

After Kari completed her B.A. at St. Olaf, she worked in a women's shelter with Lutheran Volunteer Corps for three years. Her woman's voice and advocacy role had been finding strength so a master's in public health at Clark University was a logical next step. From there she joined the staff of Family Health International in Bangkok, Thailand working on AIDS projects. When she entered the University of North Carolina's doctoral program, she was on her way to research the impact of AIDS on women and children in Tanzania. It should be noted that although Kari was at UNC/Chapel Hill, her Duke hat was ever present for basketball games.

At twenty-one, Kurt had already discovered that his imagination could find theatrical outlets. He had worked sound and light for the Northfield Arts Guild productions from the time he turned sixteen. Now he could pursue it further. A doctorate in folklore seemed to be his answer taking him back to the same building where his dad had spent so much time in African history studies at Indiana University.

Not long after Kurt started his doctoral studies, he described a moment in the library. Guided, perhaps, by his dad's presence in their shared University setting, he googled Gerald Walter Hartwig. Up came screen after screen listing articles, books and reviews that he'd written. Suddenly, it seemed to be a new coming of age as he sat glued to the screen. His dad. They were sharing the same space.

With each of the kids completing their several degrees and discovering new possibilities, a suggestion from a University of Minnesota professor that I consider doctoral studies made sense. Here I was, teaching and advocating with absolutely no credentials other than experience. Now that my primary family financial obligations were over, maybe it was time to consider this. As I was soon heading to Durham with students for the January term, I planned to confer with my mentor, John Hope Franklin.

A distinguished professor at Duke, John Hope Franklin had come to St. Olaf in 1981 to give a series of lectures. During that visit, he offered to help me with my Durham contacts. Over the next eight years, he and Aurelia, his wife, hosted me with my students for a meal in their home. Their hospitality and counsel had evolved into a treasured friendship.

But then, the phone call came, three weeks into my Durham Interim stay. When my niece, Kava – Peg's daughter – called to say, "It's Gus," I knew, of course. Only the circumstances distinguished his sudden and untimely death. Skiing with his daughter Lis and husband, Mike, one moment he stood upright, the next he fell into the snow.

My first thought was only one word, "Mom." Not only did I need to get home as fast as possible, I had to arrange for the students to complete their final week in Durham. I wouldn't meet with John Hope.

This time, I would have to tell Charlotte by myself. I would have to do so as quickly as possible or she would hear it from others including the media. Gus was a Minnesota presence of significance. As a former state finance commissioner and now Vice-President Treasurer at the University of Minnesota, his sudden death at age sixty-one would be front page news in the Minneapolis Star Tribune and on the local TV news stations.

Charlotte's caretakers went to her room immediately. They unplugged her television, telling her it was broken. No visitors were able to see her until I could get there. I did bring kringla, wine and a candle. How much more sorrow could this ninety-five-year-old mother absorb? If there is grace in short-term memory loss, she needed as much generosity of forgetting as possible.

Some months later, however, when several of Gus's family came for a visit, Charlotte looked at us entering her room and turning to me, she asked, "Has anyone else died lately?"

I had already become aware that I was perceived in the Northfield community as a woman whose primary identifier was written on my forehead - loss. But now, even my Mom saw me as the bearer of family tragedy.

Would there be no end to these sudden and untimely deaths? Not long after Gus, Bruce Benson, our college pastor, stopped me on campus, took my hand and said, "You have to be really tired of all this."

What I seemed to be learning was that there was no time line for my many complex exercises. Yet, in the midst of this accumulating loss, an undercurrent of a hum persisted.

REMEMBERING

"How many children do you have?" It is a common question asked when we meet someone for the first time, especially where women are present. After introductions, it can quickly follow as an easy entre to a continuing conversation. Or not.

For years, I would choose my answer to this question depending on whom, when and where it was asked. If the question came during one of those getting-to-know-you settings, where we were complete strangers with one another, I would usually say, 'three' because I didn't want to explain. More often than not, I'd learned that saying 'four' quickly brought the conversation to an uncomfortable silence.

However, when I was in Tanzania, I didn't hesitate. In that setting, the reality of one child not living in the present was not unusual. It would be incomprehensible for a mama not to include all her children, bringing all of them to the present. If she didn't, her child was indeed dead.

This folktale, "The Cowtail Switch", comes from Liberia. When we included it in "Are You Listening?" I couldn't have imagined how these wise words would someday speak to me.

The Cowtail Switch

Near the edge of the Liberian rain forest, on a hill overlooking the Cavally River, was the village of Kundi. Its rice and cassava fields spread in all directions. Cattle grazed in the grassland near the river. Smoke from the fires in the round clay houses seeped through the palm leaf roofs and from a distance these faint columns of smoke seemed to hover over the village. Men and boys fished in the river with nets, and women pounded grain in wooden mortars before their houses.

In this village, with his wife and many children, lived a hunter by the name of Ogaloussa. One morning, Ogaloussa took his weapons down from the wall of his house and went into the forest to hunt. His wife and his children went to tend their fields, and drove their cattle out to graze. The day passed, and they ate their evening meal of manioc and fish. Darkness came, but Ogaloussa did not return.

Another day went by, and still Ogaloussa didn't come back. They talked about it and wondered what could have detained him. A week passed, then a month. Sometimes Ogaloussa's sons mentioned that he hadn't come home. The family cared for the crops, and the sons hunted for game, but after a while they no longer talked about Ogaloussa's disappearance.

Then, one day, another son was born to Ogaloussa's wife. His name was Puli.

Puli grew older. He began to sit and to crawl. The time came when Puli began to talk, and the first thing he said was, "Where is my father?"

The other sons looked across the rice fields. "Yes one of them said," Where is Father?" "He should have returned a long time ago," another one said." Something must have happened," said another.

And so the sons took their weapons and started to look for Okaloosa. The forest was dark and many times they lost their way. At last they came to clearing and there on the ground lay Okaloussa's bones and his rusted weapons.

Then each son stepped forward to say how he would give him life. One said, "I know how to put his bones together." Another said, "I know how to cover his skeleton with sinews and flesh." Another said, "I can put breath into his body," and then another said, "I can give him the power of speech," and another, "I can give movement to his body."

When they finished, Ogaloussa looked around said, "Let us return to our home." After several days, a cow was killed for a great feast. He took the cow's tail and braided it, then decorated it with beads and cowry shells. It was beautiful. Ogaloussa carried it with him to all-important ceremonies and everyone exclaimed that it was more beautiful than any other. Everyone hoped they might receive the cowtail switch.

One day, Ogaloussa said, "A long time ago I went into the forest where I was killed by a leopard. Then my sons came for me and they brought me back from the land of the dead. I will give this cowtail switch to one of my sons, the one who did the most to bring me home."

Then the sons began to argue between themselves; each one claimed he did the most important thing for their father. Finally, Ogaloussa asked them to be quiet. He walked over to Puli, his youngest son and said, "To this son I will give the cowtail switch, for I owe most to him."

Then all the villagers and the other sons remembered Puli's first words were, "Where is my father?" They knew Ogaloussa was right for there is a saying that a man is not dead until he is forgotten.

In our remembering, we can focus on what a loved one did, or said or didn't say or do. When that focus frames our relationships, it is difficult to let go of the hurts, the blame, the anger, the regrets. Expectations rule. But if our relationship is primary, one that can let go of the hurts, the blame, the anger, what remains is the God presence in the one whom we called and continue to call by name. It is a wise way to live for it is life transforming. Yet this understanding of choosing life isn't easy.

How and what we remember can become a cipher for who we are. For our family, two distinct characteristics named each death. One, its sudden occurrence and the other, too soon in life's anticipated years yet to live. I call it the SUDS syndrome: Sudden Untimely Death Syndrome.

Our family necrology shows how generations and age at death illustrate this all too clearly.

Grandmother Marvick	35
Melburn Donhowe	44
Jule Zabawa	53
Audrey Donhowe	49
Karl Hartwig	16
Jerry Hartwig	45
Betty Ann Ramseth	64
Gus Donhowe	61

Their names, standing alone, only tell a part of our story. Each one named in this necrology left many to live without their presence.

Grandma Anna Marvick left husband, Joseph, and children - Olive, Lula, Severt, Ida, Charlotte and Anna.

Melburn Donhowe left wife, Charlotte, and children - Peggy, Betty Ann, Jack, Gus and me

Jule Zabawa left wife, Peggy and children - Kava, Mary and Kristin

Audrey Donhowe left husband, Jack, and children - John, Erik, Rolf, Maren, Mark and Dan

117

Karl Hartwig left parents, Jerry and me, and siblings - Kristopher, Kari and Kurt

Jerry Hartwig left me, and children - Kristopher, Kari and Kurt

Betty Ann Ramseth left husband, Rudy, and children - Mark, Peter, Steve, Melinda and Gregg

Gus Donhowe left wife, Ruth, and children - Margit, Lis and Michael

From our beginnings, sudden loss has relentlessly shattered each family's sense of living with dying, of living with absence. Yet throughout all the turmoil, our sense of belonging has stayed firm. Life still has meaning, not grounded in pious platitudes, but in each parent's struggles with their five-finger exercises, for themselves, and their children. Learning how to practice resurrection is our life- line; it is our vocation. As our sorrow capacity deepens, so, too, is our capacity to cherish life.

One of the problems with SUDS is that there is no time for goodbyes; there's no time to say forgive me, to say I love you, to say thank you. We're left with too many what if's or if only's. There's no time for unfinished business, which means we're left with grief for ourselves as well as those not present. Getting stuck is easy.

Karl's death was the result of a car accident. One of the immediate inquiries of the police was to determine if alcohol or drugs were contributing factors as the driver of the car was at fault. Duane, Karl's driver-friend, didn't see or misjudged the truck advancing around the bend as he pulled out of the gas station to the highway. There was no evidence of substance abuse. It was Duane's judgment that cost him his life and Karl's.

In 1977, lawsuits were in the early stages of becoming common redress for wrongful deaths. When Duane's family lawyer met with us within weeks of the accident, the first question was, "Do you plan to sue the family?" We were speechless, for it had not even come to our consciousness as a possibility. In any case, we'd certainly not talked about it.

I have been very grateful these many years for Jerry's wisdom at a time when rational thinking was mostly absent. By declining the suit possibility, we were freed from two things: blame and money. Karl went on this trip with our blessing, which meant that we shared responsibility. We were required to accept a minimal insurance settlement of $30,000. Dividing it between our three kids to use for their education freed us from blaming. It freed Karl's spirit to live on in their learning, in all of our remembering.

There's a profound impact of space related to those who have gone before. Traditionally, cemeteries have provided that primary remembering place. For Karl, even in the midst of those first trauma filled days, we knew his ashes needed to be spread outdoors.

Our dear friend and neighbor, Fred White, manager of Duke Forest, kindly agreed to find the right place for Karl. This is what he wrote.

Thoughts on the Forest Site

This is not the traditional sort of a spot, replete with stream and now venerable trees. The forest here is highland. It has felt the plough and the ax, and knows of the short cycles of short cycles of man and the longer cycles of its kind. It is now, quietly beginning again. Rooted in rock and with room to grow it is a young stand, vigorous and well established. Its future is that of the oaks...grand and enduring.   .

This, for Karl, it seems to me, to be fitting and very important.

With Love,

Fred

THOUGHTS ON THE FOREST SITE

THIS IS NOT THE TRADITIONAL SORT OF A
SPOT, REPLETE WITH STREAM AND NOW
VENERABLE TREES. THE FOREST HERE IS
HIGHLAND. IT HAS FELT THE PLOUGH
AND THE AX, AND KNOWS OF THE
SHORT CYCLES OF MAN AND THE LONGER
CYCLES OF ITS KIND. IT IS NOW, QUIETLY,
BEGINNING AGAIN, ROOTED IN ROCK AND
WITH ROOM TO GROW IT IS A YOUNG
STAND, VIGEROUS AND WELL ESTABLISHED.
ITS FUTURE IS THAT OF THE OAKS....
GRAND AND ENDURING.

THIS, FOR KARL, IT SEEMED TO
ME, TO BE FITTING, AND VERY
IMPORTANT.

WITH LOVE,

FRED

Cemeteries are sacred places where those who go before are remembered, their names carved in stone. They stand, collectively, immoveable, testifying to a time before. A forest site, however, is alive in the grandeur of living trees; its memories are nameless. Jerry's place in Northfield's Oaklawn cemetery has a reservation next to it for me, when my 'timely' time comes. On my stone, the carved names of all my children will remember.

Plants and flowers are part of cemetery protocol. Jerry's Mom would call periodically to ask how I was tending her son's grave. This was not in my experience since we moved from Story City when I was so little. I never observed Charlotte visiting my Dad's gravesite. But I could take flowers to Jerry's grave. It seemed relatively easy as assignments go.

Several years after his death, however, a new possibility emerged. I had gone to the nursery looking for flowers to plant in our window boxes, and there they were - geraniums. Jerry loved to garden, but geraniums were never included. In fact, he seemed to have a distinct aversion to them. I don't know what it was, the color, or maybe the aroma. He never said. All I know is that geraniums never gained admittance to our lawn or inside our home.

I bought not one but two potted geranium plants that day. As I drove to the cemetery, my conversation with Jerry was something like this. "You know, this is just too much. Why, just why did you have to die? You REALLY make me MAD!"

Getting out of my car and marching to his grave, a geranium in each hand, I summarily plopped each one on his grave as if to say, "So there!" When I tell my kids, "It's a geranium day," there is humor midst the pathos in our coded understanding.

As a folklore doctoral candidate, Kurt chose to write about this. A fellow student who read the published piece came up to him and said,

"Your mother is seriously weird." His response: "You have no idea!"

Although our many family cemetery settings offer a particular place where remembering is held, we have discovered that there are many other ways to call our memories into the present whether individually or collectively.

There are names in the new generation, names carrying the spirits of Audrey, Gerald Walter and Elizabeth Ann into the future. There are food celebrations from the need to smell kringla baking to Karl's tacos and Jerry's curry. There are magnolia tree plantings in Durham, St. Olaf scholarships, the Donhowe Building at the University of Minnesota, caftans, pottery, bow ties, roses, 'Ave Verum' and *A Sonata for Four Hands*, all remembering.

As a family with our significant crowd of witnesses, we were learning that however and whenever we remembered, we did so within a death denying culture where we are permitted a six-month time frame to – get over it.

Perhaps it is no surprise that my doctoral dissertation focused on the impact of world- view on the re-identification process for widows. My comparative study included Jewish, African American and Anglo women who were in their forties with dependent children.

If I could choose my mourning group, it would be the Jewish community. Not only do they understand grieving, they ritualize the public process with *kadish*. For a year, those bereaved stand at the close of Sabbath service, acknowledging the absence of a loved one. By so doing, the community is charged with responsibility to be present, to gradually walk them back to life where they can dare to exhale once again.

There is no timeline for remembering or for its sudden, unexpected surprises. Two Christmases ago, our family was gathered with Kari and her husband, Dennis. Under the tree was a big box with grandson Nathan's name on it. To our amazement, it held his Grandpa Jerry's London Fog Coat. Now this coat had a story. Somehow, after Jerry's death, I couldn't part with it so it hung in our hall closet next to Karl's favorite jean jacket.

One day when Kurt was in high school, he looked at his Dad's coat and tried it on. "Hey, Mom," he said, stretching out his arms, "it fits!" And so the London Fog left our closet. Years later, when Kari and Dennis were visiting Kurt and his wife Lisa, Kurt asked Dennis if he would like it because he no longer wore it. Realizing the coat memory, Dennis agreed.

But after several years, he thought that perhaps the grandson might like the coat. Nathan didn't miss a beat as he took the London Fog out of the box. He put it on, stretching out his still growing arms, and said, "Cool!"

Later that night, when Kurt, Lisa and I returned home, I went to my hall closet, took out Karl's favorite jean jacket and put it on. And then I wrote this-

A TALE OF TWO COATS

A faded blue denim jacket

With sheepskin lining

His favorite

His second skin

Just right with blue jeans

  Tennis shoes

  Just right for a teenager

But then

One night

His favorite coat

His second skin

Just hung in the Closet

The one by the front door

Except for the nights his little brother

Huddled under the denim jacket

Pleading, "He has to come back,

Just to say goodbye!"

A London Fog

With zip out lining

Drab olive green

Long enough sleeves

Just right with desert boots

   Just right for a prof

         Even a dean

But then

One night

The London Fog hung in the Closet

The one by the front door

Right next to the Blue Denim jacket

With sheepskin lining

Year after year

They hung together

The Denim jacket and the London Fog

They hung together

In the Closet

Next to the front door

Ten years later

The little brother

The youngest child

Saw the coat

The London Fog

Hanging in the Closet

He tried it on

The arms were long enough

Just right

For a growing son

With tennis shoes

Just right

                        For a memory wearing son

And so the London Fog left

The Hall Closet

Until one day

Years later

The London Fog was hanging

In the son's closet

Right next to his front door

He asked his brother- in- law,

"Would you like to wear this coat?"

Hesitant yet

Wanting to do the right thing

He took the coat

For several years

It was just right

Until one day

  He asked the growing up grandson

First year college student

"Would you like to wear this coat?"

                        The grandson tried on the London fog

Sleeves long enough

It was just right

"Cool," he said

        Even with *malapas*

Now the blue jean jacket

With the sheepskin lining

Had been hanging in the closet

Right next to the front door

All by itself

  It had been hanging there

For thirty-four years

But when the grandson tried on the London Fog

His grandma went to her Closet

The one by the front door

She took out the Blue Denim jacket

Her son's jacket with sheepskin lining

His second skin

She tried it on

Thirty-four years later

It was just right

But only

once

in

a

while

There is life remembering that line our coats and so many other objects that call out memories. Sometimes, the lining is seamless and other times it is shredded. Sometimes, there are holes filled with so much sadness, we can't put on the coat. In fact, we don't have a coat to put on; we try not to remember.

This was true for Charlotte and the remembering of her father, Joseph Marvick who died at the age of fifty-nine, her brother, Severt at age twenty-seven and sister, Ida, at age forty-one. Their names were clouded with more silence than words.

Joseph's decision that his children would attend St. Olaf for their college degrees seemed full of promise. What he couldn't have imagined was his beloved son becoming ill with tuberculosis because his roommate was already infected. Nor could he have imagined that Ida's marriage would quell this gifted daughter's spirit and voice. He had forbidden her marriage to an Ole because there was evidence that someone in his family had tuberculosis.

Rumors of Ida's abusive marriage were such that Joseph decided he had to see for himself. He drove to Randall, not far from Story City. We do not know what he saw or what Ida said. What we do know is this. It was late afternoon. He told Ida he felt like going for a walk, but could she give him a paper and pencil, because he had some things on his mind he might want to write down. And, could she give him her husband's pistol because he might see some crows.

When Joseph didn't return for supper, Ida sent Walter, her husband, to look for him. It didn't take long to discover Joseph. He had shot himself after writing an eloquent letter to his parents and children, begging forgiveness. The weight, the sorrow he carried as Severt's death became imminent and Ida's life was crumbling was more than he could bear.

In his suicide note, Joseph said very clearly that he believed he was the cause of these tragedies. He was responsible. He believed he had sinned beyond mercy and forgiveness. Three daughters were pregnant at the time – Lula, Ida and Charlotte. How could this have happened?

The church, the community, the family responded to this inexplicable tragedy in particular ways. The pastor of the church certainly knew Joseph, knew of his faithful role as a father to his children over twenty years. He also knew him to be a faithful churchman. The pastor's willingness to have a church service at that time, in 1918, was contrary to the teachings of the church.

The editor of the Story City Herald wrote a lengthy obituary, citing several of Joseph's colleagues who noticed an increasing sense of withdrawn like depression. In reflecting about his leadership in the community over so many years, there was gratitude expressed, not censure.

For the family, it wasn't that easy. Living in Story City meant that Olive and Charlotte's families had to face friends and neighbors daily with assumptions of what people were thinking.

Given the relationship between my dad and mom, I like to imagine that it was my dad's strength, counsel and love that kept mom on a steady keel. Anna, who had just finished her first year at St. Olaf, never returned because of the shame she felt.

There could be no dodging the shame for all of them. I was forty-two before I knew this unbelievably sad story. Mom simply never spoke about it. Unutterable silence. My sister Peg knew because some of her cousins who grew up in Story City had told her. Somehow, it didn't keep her out of the race.

The pain, the shame, the overwhelming sadness of Severt, Ida and Joseph's stories seemed beyond speech. I did give them life in Charlotte's memoir, *Sonata for Four Hands*, but I did so only after her death. That she silenced this memory was her way of living with it. I honored her decision. But to write her story without including this overwhelming sadness would be to leave out a very significant part of her race - how she continued to choose life.

As a single woman these many years, I think about Joseph's Story City world. Whom did he have to talk with those many years as a single man raising six children? With whom could he dare bare his soul? And who might have talked with him about his damning understanding of sin that could have changed his decision?

For the Marvick family, this remembering was impossible. The only way to live with Joseph's death was dead silence. But for our family, we have been learning to live with absence, each of us, in our own way. Remembering keeps memory alive. Remembering reminds us of goodness and kindness. It tells us who we are and to whom we belong. Endings and beginnings.

June 20, 2008 would have been my 50th wedding anniversary. Maybe it was because other family members in my age group had celebrated grandly. Because Kristopher, Kari and I were in Tanzania at the time, they planned a quiet evening to remember their dad and me. This is what Kristopher wrote:

On the Occasion of

Remembering   *Mom and Dad*

    Getting married 50 years ago

    I think of

Complex rhythms

    How Love and Dreams and Grace

      Beat together

Love that became also

    Family and Vocation

    Keeping us moving and loving

     Up to now

Dreams

    Some living   *Some dying*

    But there is a drumbeat

It keeps us moving

    As some dreams grow

  And root and become alive

    Surprising Rhythms

Amazing Rhythms of Grace

    Too much beyond understanding

    Yet enfolding us   Always

A love bigger than ours

    Complexity without Knowing

      Gratitude

        Kristopher June 2008

The gift of words and the gift of a Tanzanite ring marked this remarkable day. When I returned to the States, my left hand was no longer bereft. Another transposing of rings.

    If God did indeed become flesh and dwell among us for all time -

        how are we to know?

A SONG IS FOR SINGING

What is it to live and to die? This question, those words that first found life on the yellow tablet, they are now forty years old. When I wrote them, I was forty-one. At my most recent birthday gathering, Kristopher raised his wine glass, looked at me and asked with a twinkle: "So Mom, what's your ten-year plan?"

The first thing that came to mind was this: "I don't have a bucket list; no travel desires. But, I'm very aware of how important it is to care for my mind, body and spirit." Of course I kept thinking about the question, so here's my more carefully thought out answer:

To be mindful of my mind, body and spirit

so that I can continue to live fearlessly

because I am extravagantly loved

The words *daring to live once again* are now thirty-nine years old. One of the loss lessons I've come to understand is the lack of control in life management. The human need to do so is timeless. Finding meaning in this knowledge is at the heart of living fearlessly for at its core is amazement, is possibility. However, it's a difficult song to sing.

This knowing doesn't take away my sense of vulnerability. Over these many years as I continued to enter arenas of knowledge and life experiences after Jerry's death at St. Olaf, my role as a teacher, program facilitator and as a single parent were not separate. What I was discovering was how the many beats in my life were part of the same composition, a vocation of discovery.

In 1985, I was meeting faculty at the University of Dar es Salaam who were interested not only in our new program but in my earlier '60s history at Ilboru Secondary School. Out of this grew a request. Since I was Lutheran, might I be willing to visit a few secondary schools now managed by the Tanzanian Lutheran church. Introductions to two diocese Bishops were written.

For the next ten years, I continued to begin my Tanzanian trip at the University and then travel up country to the Arusha and Moshi regions, listening to increasing numbers of teachers throughout the country.

I had no idea what I was doing. At each school, I asked the same question to begin the discussion: "What do you need that would make a difference in your teaching?" It seemed to be a first. Over the years, the school requests increased so that I was traveling to five regions of Tanzania. I traveled extensively, listened intently and then returned to Minnesota and St. Olaf.

After each trip, I'd report to the headquarters of the church in Tanzania and the US. In 1995, I received a request that I move to Tanzania and facilitate this new emerging partnership between these two national churches. The teachers had named this fledgling organization –Mwangaza Education for Partnership ELCT/ELCA. Mwangaza is a Kiswahili word meaning enlightenment. Named by teachers, it continues to show us how educational partnerships can bring new life to all participants.

The timing was right. The kids were well launched. We had conferred deciding that they would back me in this next venture. The Northfield house sold and my downsized belongings were put into storage.

In 1996, I moved to a house on the same road that Jerry and our two babes bumped over thirty-five years before. By now, the Psalm's words *'you have rescued my soul from death, my feet from stumbling so that I walk before God in the light of the living* were inscribed in my heart daring me to be fearless once again.

Our Mwangaza Centre, located at the end of the road next to Ilboru Secondary School, continues as the operational headquarters for our outreach. Another full circle. Our partnership model, linking twenty regions of both international churches, is now twenty years old. Our three seminar offerings for teachers, mothers and daughters and congregational men and women are well established and highly sought throughout the country.

Over the years, participants have guided us towards topics that could change their lives. This means that HIV/AIDS, gender- based violence, bullying, parenting, women's health, conflict resolution, water borne diseases are included along with professional development learning. We call this approach- Literacy for Living -realizing that knowing is the first step. Becoming change agents requires practice in finding your own advocacy voice with others.

From our beginnings, we have described ourselves as a grassroots, faith based organization. Although we are Lutheran and organizationally linked to the twenty companion synods and dioceses of the Evangelical Lutheran Church in Tanzania with the Evangelical Lutheran Church in America, we welcome Christian, Muslim and traditional believers.

We started providing seminars for teachers in secondary schools, knowing that the majority of the church managed schools lacked sufficient texts and learning resources. When I first went to Tanzania in 1961, less than one percent of teenagers were admitted to secondary schools. Today, the percentage is a mere seven percent. The national examination pass rate is only in the thirty per cent quartile.

Because English is the language of instruction, the majority of students and too many teachers are challenged. English is their third language. Lack of reading materials doesn't help. Mwangaza is changing that with the introduction of mini-books. If you fold an 8 x 11 paper twice – you have a book. We have written seven books for each grade level, beginning with a contextual story but then centering on difficult parts of the high school syllabus.

They were so successful, that seven books were written in Swahili for the other two seminar offerings – Binti-Mama or Mother Daughter and Congregational leaders. Because all seminar participants are prepared to return to their respective environments and teach others, they use these books as aids. Annually, we 'publish' off of our copy machine about a thousand mini-books. What we have come to understand through Mwangaza is that literacy is much more than reading and understanding words.

Collaboration, cooperation, relationships and hospitality are Mwangaza's foundation. The operation at our Centre and all seminar offerings are team centered. John Kavishe, Salome Lally and Nemayan King'ori are the management team. Decisions are shared. The Mwangaza Board in Tanzania reviews their program planning and their budget annually. Friends of Mwangaza, Inc. the 501 (c) (3) stateside board seeks funds and volunteers to support our outreach.

Mwangaza has had two godmothers and one godfather these

twenty years. Lynda Tidemann Minnick and Lois Leffler guided, mentored and supported us every month of the way. Mchungaji Gabrieli Kimirei, bears a title of 'shepherd-pastor' in Swahili He was Jerry's and my student way back when we taught at Ilboru Secondary School. That he chose to shepherd Mwangaza as our Tanzanian Board Chair was an inestimable gift, professionally and personally. I couldn't have done it without them.

Now it is the Tanzanian leadership that provides the enlightened support for our outreach. Their imaginations have been ignited not only in creative responses to ongoing requests, but the sustaining of our unique collaborative partnership. Their presence brings Tanzanians and Americans into a Mwangaza space where learning is discovered together.

When I accepted the Mwangaza position and moved to Tanzania in 1996, all by myself, I was sixty years old. "What are you going to do after this?" became a fairly common question. My initial response, "I plan to write, " hasn't changed. Nights can be long in Tanzania with darkness religiously appearing at 7 p.m., always. At first, poetry emerged. Once I started, it seemed that words had been queuing over the years, waiting for life on the page. This is one.

SHOONIE HARTWIG

THANKSGIVING

Pain is missed in Praise

It's the only time

    I've disagreed

        With Emily

            Dickenson

                That is

But then if she'd been here

    Where pain is not missed in praise

Not like at home

    Where we work so very hard

        To walk on top of pain

        To deny suffering

    Ignore it away   Drink it away Exercise it away Praise it away

Where praise is on a grid of answers

    No Questions

    Not a Rilke response

When faith knows but dares not feel

    When faith knows but denies vulnerability

        When faith knows but insists on its own way

God forgive us

    For then

    From what source is

    Our praise   Our healing   Our thanksgiving

Here

    Pain is part of praise   Sorrow is part of joy

    Life is part of death   Mystery is part of revelation

        Nospaces

Except for the gouged valleys

Except for thanksgiving

    Erupting out of the depths

    Of pain

        Not missed

            In praise

Shukrani

    Thanksgiving

    For seeing the Face of God

        One   More   Day

For

        A safe journey   Every morsel of food Rain

For

        A malaria cure   A healed relationship   A book

Pain is so searing   Praise is so exultant

        Nothing is missed

          In

        Praise

I didn't finish Charlotte's memoir, *Sonata for Four Hands* until I returned to the States. Two years ago, I completed *Education of a Stranger.* The cover, designed by my son-in-law Dennis, shows three trees – a Norway pine, a North Carolina magnolia and a Tanzanian baobab, illustrating the three sources of stories – three beats.

Using a lexicon format, each of the twelve sections begins with a Swahili word such as 'wanawake na watoto' (women and children), or 'elimu' (education), or 'njaa' (hunger) demonstrating the distance between the two not only in language but how our initial spaces of 'knowing' what these words mean have similar yet different understandings within other settings. The stories illuminating my stranger education show how I have been carefully and wondrously taught.

When this manuscript, *Living with Dying,* is finished, the cover is ready. When I asked Dennis for another watercolor design, his question, "What do you imagine?" brought this response: "A caked desert with springs of green." It's perfect.

Next is a collaborative writing project about Aniceti Kitereza, whom we met during our stay on the island of Ukerewe. His is an amazing story. From that sequestered, remote part of Tanzania comes his epic novel completed in 1945. Written in his own language, Kikerebe, he wrote to preserve the ways of his people with this as his focus – what should we teach our children?

When Jerry read the first chapters, he knew that this was a literary find. Initial publishing contacts in Tanzania would not consider *Myombekere na Buganoka* until it was translated into Kiswahili, all 350 typewritten pages. The story of the following ten years in letters between Kitereza, Heinemanns in Nairobi, translator in Arusha, Catholic Fathers on Ukerewe, Jerry in Durham, N.C. and Emilie Larson in Boston, MA is an epistolary saga.

It was not until 1982 that Kitereza's book was finally published in Swahili. It has subsequently been translated and published into English, German and French. Yet, the name Aniceti Kitereza is not known well in his own country outside of University literature classes. Not only is his book the longest epic ever written in the continent of Africa, it ranks alongside the Leaky Olduvai Gorge discovery of the first humanoid as a first in global literature. **Aniceti Kitereza – A Tanzania Epic** tells the story of this extraordinarily ordinary man. I am collaborating with St. Olaf, Tanzanian professor, Joseph Mbele.

Two other writing projects are in the queue. This title: *The Measure of a Man – a Hartwig Yardstick –* I've known for years. Jerry's dad operated the Hartwig Hardware store in Brush, Colorado where yardsticks were sold with Hartwig inscribed. I still have ours as well as letters kept by his parents from college to our years in Tanzania.

Wading in the Water has me going in circles. Literally. My church, Redeemer Lutheran, is located in north Minneapolis, where Black Lives Matter challenges us all. As a faith community and as an Old White Woman, the myriad intersections of location and advocacy are pushing me into the troubled word waters of local and global. There is this new term, glocal, but as yet, I have not seen or heard how we might truly discover those connections. As people of faith, what narratives do we speak, sing, pray as we join hands with all of God's people?

Hence, there are three circles, each with a theme. The first is 'Doing Justice' – Foreign/Domestic. The second is 'Loving Kindness' – Faith/Creed and the third is 'Walking Humbly' – Point of View. At present, my reading includes – *Raging with Compassion, Bonhoeffer's Black Jesus, Troubling Biblical Waters, The Third Reconstruction, Just Mercy, Evicted and America's Original Sin.*

Yes, a song is for singing. When I wrote these words not long after Karl's death, I couldn't have imagined how many would sing for me when I couldn't utter a sound. Nor could I have imagined how many new songs I would learn from others.

A Song is for Singing

When life seems to be just a desert of sand
When flowers you pick are only thorns in your hand
When your shadow is lost and there's only night
Where is the courage to seek, to look for the light?

Is a song, a song for singing?
Is life, is life for living?
Is love, is love for giving, for giving?

Jesus sits with you brother, he knows your pain.
Jesus sits with you sister, he renews life again.
When you know that light that turns the night into day
You'll keep on finding ways to give your love away

Yes, a song, a song's for singing
And life, yes life's for living
And love, love is for giving, for giving.

The opening piano chord is a c minor diminished 7th. This is an unfinished, an unsettled chord, seeking resolution. Like life. Although I wrote this several months after Karl's death, over these many years, my hands are drawn to this piece more than any other. It eked out of the pillar to resurface throughout my lifetime tutorial of losing and living as I began to live my particular suffering story.

Suffering stories are ageless; they are timeless - from Scriptures, to folk tales, to academic works, to personal, written testimonies. One Hasidic folk tale, 'The Sorrow Tree,' tells it this way.

The Sorrow Tree

There was a time, the story says, when everyone complained to their neighbors about their trials and tribulations. Each one affirmed their sufferings to be worse than anyone else. Their prayers, their demands of God were incessant. Finally, God brought all his people together and said:

"For this one day, I am giving you freedom from all your trials, from your weeping and wailing. But this you must do. Go to my garden where you will find The Great Sorrow Tree. You will find the branches heavy with people's stories from all time. Hang your stories there as well. Read all of them carefully because by sunset, you must choose the sorrow best suited for you."

And so God's people read and read. They read of famine, of devastation, of war, of unspeakable brutality. They read of desolation, of loneliness, of abandonment. All day long, they read.

At sunset, not one took another's sorrow. Each one of God's people kept theirs.

Suffering is at the core of being human. It is within the mystery of our particular suffering stories that life reveals new meaning. This is where our questions of 'Who is God?' and 'Why?' give shape to our theology, our living, our relationships. Indeed, our family sorrow tree is loss heavy. Yet we have learned how to sing new songs because we have been extravagantly loved.

Charlotte's sorrow tree started when she was three years old. She lived almost 103 years. It's a long time to be the tree trunk, especially given its many weighted boughs. Her purposeful stride began to falter in her mid-nineties. The transitions between her independent walking to walker to wheelchair were short. Once she had no piano bench, her world became smaller and quieter. It seemed that she had completed all her races.

The rest of us are still running. Kristopher and Rebecca's home is often in overflow whether it is their children and grands, friends, refugees or someone needing a safe, hospitable space. Kristopher heads the Hospice Palliative unit at the Minneapolis VA Hospital. Although Rebecca's nursing and music, carpentry and teaching keep her more than busy, the door of their home is always open.

Through the years, I've loved seeing my grands marry well, (Nate Seth and Daniel *bado*), seeing them parent my greats – Zachary Gerald, Joshua Allen, Luke Walter, Isaac Walter, William Hobbes and Bethany Charlotte is an indescribable joy.

Kari married the husband of one of my best friends. Dennis and Meredith were my neighbors on Ilboru Road during my early years at Mwangaza. When Meredith developed breast cancer, our relationship deepened as she spent treatment time in Minnesota while Dennis and sons

Chris and Jesse stayed in Tanzania.

After her death, our family friendship extended to Kari. When Dennis first asked me about her, my first response was this, "I think you might be the first person outside of our family who will understand her in that you have both suffered loss." Kari teaches in the Physicians Assistant and Global Health programs at St. Catherine's in St. Paul. Dennis paints and paints winning kudos at state and national levels. Their home continues to be our celebratory space for ordinary and extraordinary gatherings. A late afternoon call from Kari, "Hey Mom, how about a glass of wine?" brings a joyous serendipity.

Kurt, at age five, exclaimed with great dismay, "I'm beginning to lose my imagination." It was more than increasing requirements to color inside the lines. When he was not quite three, he periodically expressed the need 'to be myself'. He would go to his room, shut the door, put on his cowboy hat, gather books, put on a record ready to settle on his bed for an indefinite 'be myself' time.

I think it's fair to say, that Kurt has continuously pursued avenues of not losing it. His play writing, set designing and directing have extended to book writing. There is a noticeable theme in all of these creative avenues - a prevalence of death or loss. The mother of one of his high school friends who died at age sixteen from heart failure said, "Kurt was born with an old soul."

150

When he and Lisa Gildehaus wed, I recognized immediately that their creative spirits would feed one another. When they spoke early of their mutual passions, they named family as a shared legacy of love, care and delight. Their continuous exploration of artistic endeavors are evident in Lisa's documentary filming and Kurt's artistic directing. Whenever they are present, three ingredients are a certainty: invigorating conversation, boisterous laughter and fabulous food.

Observing my children over the years, I am a very grateful mama. I not only love them dearly, I really do like them. Their chosen professions continue to nourish and challenge each one in life giving ways. Each has married extraordinarily well as they continue to share visions and possibilities of what is yet to be. Each of their homes is notable in gentle, kind and generous spirits given freely.

Could it be that from the seeds of suffering and oppression, rejection and utter desolation, springs an inner, stronger compassion, joy and hope? For our roots have sunk deeper into the knowledge of who we really are – to whom we really belong.

What we have come to know, in part, through our family stories, is that we have joined the well- trod life paths that have no boundaries, no exclusions. Sneakers, spike heels, bare feet, boots walk. Men, women,

children, gay, straight, rich, poor walk. People of all hues, with and without
faith walk. All know suffering, the core of being human. When we
acknowledge this, no one walks separately, above or below. We walk
together. We walk with hope. We walk with possibility. We walk together.

Our family vocation is rooted in our shared experiences of absence
of presence. We have learned that there is no sparing, no righteous
exclusion. Throughout these years, we have heard others whose cries of
'My God, why have you forsaken me?' echo ours. Discovering God's
presence within the raw realities of suffering is to know a transformation
from

Absence of presence

To

Presence of absence

Martin Buber, the renowned Jewish philosopher, wrote - "The
Bond Between the Spirits," read by Kari as part of "Are You Listening?" I
rephrased it to be gender inclusive:

When we are singing and cannot lift our voice

And others come and sing with us

Others who can lift their voice

The first will be able to lift their voice, too

This is the secret

Of the bond

Between the Spirits

Born in Austria, Buber lived through the World Wars. Within his Jewish tradition, midst all the horrors he witnessed and knew, brutality, fear and betrayal could have exterminated his living. Yet the secret of the bond between the spirits is when those who are able, do not forget those who cannot. Those who are able, hum for those who are mute so that with time, they are able, once again, to find their own voice.

When the words for "A Song is for Singing" first emerged with the question – 'Is a song for singing, is life for living, is love for giving?' a thunderbolt. Yes, love is *for giving*, but love is *forgiving*.

Amazing what difference a space makes. It is here in the in-between of forgiving and for giving where I continue to learn.

It's in this space between forgiving and for giving where the pillar gives needed retreat from the madding crowd, refusing full-time residence with memories of sorrow. It is where others come and sing with us, where creative beginnings of new ways to sing fearlessly become possible.

In my early pillar residency, this space shielded me, a survival necessity. As circumstances forced me to not only leave but to dare imagine the future, the pillar became generative. Quiet. Dark. Light came when I'd dare imagine. The light, sometimes too glaring, might cause a retreat.

My pillar holds me still for it is there that I am Karl's mom, where I am Jerry's wife, where memory gently surrounds me. My pillar residency is now primarily my living space. This is where Tanzanian batiks and carvings, a Kathe Kollwitz print, family pictures, Ruth's, Jackie's and Heidi's original oil paintings, MPR and books everywhere, remind me. It is where Kari's elegant macramé filter light from the porch, where Rebecca's hand hewn curled cherry buffet holds pottery and where candles glow. The yellow tablet is transformed to a beautiful calligraphy of 'what is it to live and to die'. And, there is Charlotte's baby grand – the piano bench -lest I forget.

Buber's - 'When we are singing and cannot lift our voice' is a life secret waiting to be discovered over and over again. It requires a letting go to begin again. But not alone. When we hear the cries of another, singing for them when they are mute is a prelude to a song we can learn to sing together. And when we do, the bond between us is unshakeable.

It is in this caked, barren desert between

Forgiving   and   for giving

where we join humanity's cry

"My God, why have you forsaken me?"

This is exactly where God's ever present Spirit saves us from ourselves. Our desperation over what has been is absorbed in God – with – us. It is transposed so that our resurrected voices are able to sing with others for all that is yet to be.

We are re-membered.

This is where gratitude overflows for my beloved, for all who have taught and continue to teach me how to sing once again so that somehow I might dare to become the song.

It is here, in this forgiving, in this for giving place, where

it is possible for the desert to blossom

Karl's

mother.

AFTER WORDS

To all my beloved children – Kristopher and Rebecca, Kari and Dennis, Kurt and Lisa. To all my beloved grands – Daniel, Jenny and Jason, Kirsten and Ray, Heidi and Paul, Nate Seth Walter. To all my beloved great grands – Zachary Gerald, Joshua Allen, Bethany Charlotte, Luke Walter, William Hobbes, Isaac Walter. You keep teaching me new songs to sing all the while loving me extravagantly.

To Ludie and Fred White who walked with me through so many of these pages. Your own walk gives steadfast devotion new meaning.

To editor Patricia Francesca. You guided me to new writing spaces with insistent and gentle prodding.

To friend Janet Hagberg. You graciously brought me into Patricia's orbit.

To Dennis Murnyak and Doug Dybsetter. For the cover design, Asanteeni!

To all of my family – Hartwigs, Donhowes, Zabawas, Ramseths, Hansons, Ruppels.

For all the saints…Jubilate Deo
To all of my Mwangaza and Abiding Savior families
Mahali ni pazuri na Mungu ni pendo

A SONG IS FOR SINGING!

ABOUT THE AUTHOR

Shoonie Hartwig's publications reflect her inter- cultural living whether in Tanzania, Minnesota, North Carolina as a teacher, researcher, a facilitator of educational partnerships or as a member of multi-cultural congregations. Her books include: THE BOOK AND THE DRUM, SONATA FOR FOUR HANDS, EDUCATION OF A STRANGER and ANICETI KITEREZA – A TANZANIAN EPIC (2017).

Made in the USA
Middletown, DE
29 January 2017